The Pastoral Nature of the Ministry

THE
PASTORAL NATURE
OF THE MINISTRY

FRANK WRIGHT

SCM PRESS LTD

334 01212 0

First published 1980
by SCM Press Ltd
26–30 Tottenham Road, London N1 4BZ

Fourth impression 1986

Typeset by Gloucester Typesetting Co. Ltd
and printed in Great Britain by
Richard Clay (The Chaucer Press) Ltd,
Bungay, Suffolk

Contents

The title of this book may seem pretentious, and raise expectations which it does not fulfil. It is essentially a personal statement, my view of the pastoral nature of the ministry, arrived at through a putting together of reflections on my own experience and the wisdom, help and insights I have derived from many friends and colleagues over many years and in many places. To them, my deep gratitude, and to the reader my apologies for treating partially and inadequately a subject which takes us to the heart of our humanity and of God's love. I shall be satisfied if others treat more fully and expertly of the questions I have haltingly raised.

I

What is the Pastor For?

'Do not visit parishioners on Mondays – it's Washing Day; they will not wish to see you, and the steam can be very unpleasant.'[1] Such was the down-to-earth advice one of Dr V. A. Demant's predecessors in the Chair of Moral and Pastoral Theology in the University of Oxford used to give to his students. It was an approach to pastoral matters sanctioned by long tradition, practically and sensibly concentrating on the things to be done, and the way to do them.

It was a fellow-curate's question which made me query this approach in the first few months after my ordination, some thirty years ago – and it is a question which has haunted me ever since. At Monday morning staff-meeting we were organizing parishioners from the comfort of our armchairs: someone to take over the Brownies, supervise the envelope-scheme, help with the monthly Pram Service. 'But what,' asked my colleague, 'am I supposed to be doing with people I meet? What am I for?' Looking back now, it seems surprising that I had not asked the question, or that it had not been brought to my attention in the course of my training. But such was the assured position of the ministry then that it was felt sufficient to give instruction in the 'how' of parochial ministry: how to hold the baby when baptizing, how to conduct yourself when travelling back (upright) in the hearse after a funeral, how to avoid the perils of visiting an unmarried lady in her bed-sit. It was important to know how to use the occasional offices for evangelistic or parochial ends, how to spread the parish net still further. Ultimate questions, questions of purpose and value, questions relating to the significance of the pastoral relationship, were assumed or ignored. You got on with the job as effectively as you could.

Silence on such ultimate questions has scarcely been broken

since those days. Despite the impetus afforded by the Clinical
Theology Movement and the development in a handful of
universities and theological colleges of integrated pastoral
studies, the question as to what the minister is for as a pastor is
still largely unasked and unanswered. Of course, the question
looks foolish, and is not really a question to those for whom
parish-organization and filling the pews is all absorbing, or
those who are content with (numerically) 'building up the Body
of Christ'. Others may not need to look beyond the authority of
the ministerial priesthood conveyed to them by the grace of
ordination: others may be satisfied with their leading role as
human agents of conversion and salvation. But if (as I believe,
and from my experience a number of others, too) none of these
ways of seeing things touches the heart of the matter; if I am
called to spend my life with people in a special relationship in a
community which traditionally gives me a particular pastoral
and shepherding role, then what does that mean today, and how
am I to fulfil it? The neglect of this question is particularly
ironic in the Church of England which, partly because of its
territorial coverage, has always prided itself on its pastoral
emphasis, and its long tradition of the vicar as the 'father of the
flock'. There is no lack of handbooks on pastoral care, on how
to do those things which are an essential part of ecclesiastical
ministry, George Herbert and Richard Baxter updated to the
twentieth century. But these handbooks seem to me to assume
that I already know what I am for, and seem to be written for
stable patterns of church life, which I find to be increasingly
uncommon.

Perhaps there are three main reasons for silence about this
question. The first is our unwillingness to give proper weight
and seriousness to that discipline, so well-developed across the
Atlantic since the last war, of pastoral theology. That discipline
has most comprehensively been defined by James Lapsley as
'the study of all aspects of the care of persons in the Church in a
context of theological inquiry, including implications for other
branches of theology.'[2] For myself, I would happily omit the
words 'in the Church' as unnecessarily limiting to the scope of
the enquiry: if I am studying the care of a bereaved person,
experience suggests that that person's membership of the church
may be of much less significance than the working-out of the

sociological and psychological pattern of bereavement in his or her case. Our English slowness to respond to the challenge of pastoral theology seems to stem from a fear and distrust of what has been seen to be the godless discipline of psychology, which you can scarcely ignore if you are going to study the care of persons, together with a characteristically English pragmatic approach born of native wit and common sense (sanctified?) rather than of hard intellectual wrestling. Pastoral theology cannot appeal to those who are addicted to neat formulations: it is bound to be untidy and imprecise, an uneasy attempt at integration which must always be changing and shifting in emphasis. In the academic hierarchy, pastoral theology is seen to be the 'practical bit' at the end of other theological studies, but with a considerable gap existing between it and those other studies. Perhaps the truth may some day dawn that other forms of theology cannot be wrought in isolation from pastoral theology: if dogmatic and systematic theology does not come alive in the 'care of persons' and if pastoral theologians cannot ask pertinent questions about the meaning for human beings of statements made by dogmatic and systematic theologians all the way along, then there is deservedly little hope for theology in the future. Of course, as with all attempts at integrated studies, there is a legitimate fear that one aspect of those studies will dominate the rest, and there is some truth in the contention that 'the context of theological inquiry' has been a very pale and self-effacing context for many attempts at the writing of pastoral theology. In the USA there has been such a harnessing of psychological insights and techniques to church-based ministry that ministers often seem to have simply taken over secular counselling roles on weekdays. But if that situation is undesirable, it is no less so than the poverty-stricken spectacle of the pastoral theology shelves in the religious bookshops on this side of the Atlantic, treating as pastoral theology manuals of 'preaching at Parish Communion' in the absence of much else.

The second reason for silence has to do with professionalism in another form. If in the USA the uncertain role of the pastor has led some to be seduced by the secular-counselling role, seduction here has come from a different quarter. I have often noticed that clergy and ministers respond much better to courses of lectures and seminars on *liturgical* matters than they do on any other aspect of ministry. (I wonder now whether the priest and the Levite in the parable were not hurrying off to a liturgical conference? Their disinclination to turn their attention to pastoral matters would certainly suggest it.) The interest in devising new liturgical forms once the traditional straitjacket was burst open has provided a field-day for those whose interests lie here. It is a sad commentary on our neglect of real pastoral questions to put side by side the initiatives and energy which have gone into such provision with the small amount of interest shown in developing the inner life and spirituality of those clergy and laity who participate in such services. Indeed, for some laity liturgical reform has made the position worse. In the absence of other forms of instruction, care and nourishment, some have come to rely on the liturgy, its sense of mystery and its timelessness, for their inner nourishment. When liturgical reform was deemed to be necessary (for reasons often obscure to such laity) that source of nourishment was taken away, replaced with a much thinner diet, and lay spiritual malnutrition is even worse than before. How can you have liturgical richness without personal, inner nourishment? Revived liturgical interest has furnished the minister with a spirit of professionalism, or rather reinforced what is already present in the liturgical appeal. For despite the presence of laity, for example, on the Church of England Liturgical Commission, and despite the exhortations to laity-involvement in decisions about worship at the local church level, the area of liturgy and worship is felt by many clergy and ministers to be their one area of professional expertise. If, they feel, by virtue of our training, we do not know about worship, who does? Whatever else the helping-professions have taken over, at least that is left to us.

If it is not liturgical expertise which we feel affords us true professionalism, it may be something else. Those who have a penchant for administration will make much of the current vogue of 'church management'. In earlier days, many of us scoffed at the administrative paraphernalia required of the parish minister if he took, for instance, C. R. Forder's *Parish Priest at Work*[3] as his working guidelines. We had nightmares of a ministry based entirely on files, card-index boxes and briefcases. But they were as nothing compared with recommendations, based on sociological analyses, which are made today about how churches should be run. Of course, economy of organization and efficiency sets us free to spend time on other things, but the parallel between the church and management is an uneasy parallel (and in the last analysis, contradictory). A true professionalism is surely to be found in the pastoral ministry rather than in the smooth running of the administrative machine, which can never be more than a handmaid. An insidious debasement of ministry creeps in when administrative goals become confused with pastoral goals. The administrator-in-me wishes to empty the in-tray before the end of the working day: the pastor-in-me knows that that would be to short-circuit important personal problems which need a lot of listening to, reflection, tentative suggestion and patience – over, possibly, a long period of time. To look at my watch is a necessity if I am going to be efficient: it may be disastrous if I am to be pastorally effective.

Silence about the pastoral relationship, then, comes from a neglect of pastoral theology, and a searching for professionalism in the fields of liturgy and management. It may also, thirdly, arise from an unease with the word 'pastor', which is a trifle ironic when there has been such a multiplication of 'pastoral counsellors' in schools and elsewhere. But the words 'pastor', 'pastoral' have such a patronizing tone in these days of 'equality of opportunity' that we fight shy of using them. A reading of the classics of pastoral care soon illustrates the chief difference between the writers and ourselves: their unashamed paternalism for the gospels' sake. In this sense, there is a wider gulf of spirit between Peter Green's *Town Parson* (lectures delivered at Cambridge in 1914)[4] and our day than there is between George Herbert and Peter Green. Peter Green's early twentieth-century, industrial working-class parish in Salford was as unlike George Herbert's seventeenth-century country cure of Fugglestone with Bemerton as it could be, but he would have agreed with the confident dogmatism of George Herbert that the work of the pastor is to be 'the deputy of Christ for the reducing of Man to the obedience of God.'[5] We can be too scathing and censorious in our denunciations of paternalism. There is a thin dividing line between the gratitude felt because of friendship and good works, and the form of dependency that gratitude takes, feeding another's paternalistic spirit. In a Lancastrian parish at the time of the depression – not too dissimilar from Peter Green's Salford – when the early death of my father made life a bitter economic struggle for my mother, it was the 'good works' of the vicar which made a miserable situation more bearable. But the good works were the fruit of a strange, appealing goodness in a man who had a hyphenated name and aristocratic connections, wore a monocle, and later started a hat factory in the Panama. It was the attraction of that goodness which, I am convinced, first stirred in me the possibility of ordination. Paternalistic? Without a doubt. But sometimes we undervalue, in our ruthless zeal for clarity of motive and purpose, the effects of simple kindness and generosity.

Nevertheless, there are difficulties. It is not only that what George Herbert calls the parson's 'completeness', in which he desires to be all things to his people (pastor, lawyer – and physician!) has gone. The comparison of pastor and people with shepherd and sheep barely conceals notions completely unworthy of lay-people and sorely tempting to the ingrained authoritarian temper of clergy and ministers. Who has not known ministers ministered to by 'lay-sheep' to such an extent that when the ministers have been taken out of that supportive situation, they have sometimes gone to pieces? And they thought *they* were being the shepherd! The Good Shepherd analogy drawn from the tenth chapter of St John's gospel, on which too many of us were exclusively reared in the past, still has a lot to say of permanent importance: in particular, about the people's knowledge of the pastor which comes from his readiness to be known as a person without hiding behind a professional facade and his willingness to be available ('they know his voice') and of the commitment of pastor to people ('I lay down my life for the sheep'). But the passage has disastrous consequences for both if the analogy is pressed too narrowly. Any analogy which does not suggest that the pastoral relationship is a reciprocal relationship will not serve in the late twentieth century.

I am suggesting, then, that we should begin to penetrate the silence about the pastoral ministry of the church brought about by our refusal to take pastoral theology seriously, our searching for professionalism elsewhere and our hesitation about the patronizing and paternalistic overtones of the word 'pastoral'.

It is perhaps more than ever necessary that we ask what the pastor is for at a time when some of the traditional functions of ministry have been eroded by massive secular development in social work, the growth of professional and voluntary counselling-agencies, and the loss of ministerial status due to its poor financial reward and greater educational equality in the population at large. We Christians, of course, often feel threatened if we cannot see a Christian 'distinctiveness' for our involvements: we feel uneasy unless we can claim a uniqueness for Christ, an all-important difference between our faith and that of other world-religions, an extra perspective and resources that are denied to 'mere humanists'. Pretensions to imperialism are often a sign of insecurity – but why need we be anything than glad that, for instance, parallels between the aims of the social worker and those of the minister as pastor can be very close? Why should we grudgingly search for 'the little something extra that the others haven't got', as the old petrol advertisement had it? Rather, perhaps, we should be flattered if we look at the way in which the theory and practice of modern social services have derived from the traditional pastoral methods which the church at her best has employed. Paul Halmos in his classic work, *The Faith of the Counsellors* illustrates how social workers may only verbally confess to a 'mere technique, an elaborate professional etiquette, or a sheer casuistry of professionalised neighbourliness' but in practice their 'dedication, persistence and unthinking affection confess to much more'. 'In his labours the counsellor seems to be guided by an aspiration, by a highminded conception of what his client might become and should become. By persevering in his efforts to help, the counsellor seems to make a point, take a stand and declare for hope. At a time when, according to all common sense standards, the client appears incorrigibly useless, the counsellor is, in fact, saying, "You are worthwhile!" and "I am not put off by your illness!" '[6] How little different this is from what any pastor with Christian insight and resources would wish to say, and how much it reduces to size those exclusive Christian claims, which are often made, to 'perseverance in hopeless cases, because of Christian resources'.

One attractive answer to the question, 'What am I for?' might be a very negative answer. We might wish to argue that we are not *for* anything, that we are not here to do anything to anybody, or to engage in frenetic activity to bring in the Kingdom of God through our own breathless efforts – but simply to be. If, we might say, we are, despite all our inadequacies, 'abiding in Christ', continuously nourishing our relationship with him through attention to prayer, then we will creatively be reproducing his stance in our circumstances and the rest will follow. There is some truth here, and this position safeguards the necessity for spontaneity and lack of scrupulosity in any worthwhile ministry. In denying any goals, it reduces the temptation to manipulation. I remember being brought up sharply by a blunt Yorkshire matron who accused me of being able to 'coax ducks off water' – and of course, the more I care about building up the Body of Christ, the greater my devotion to the church, the more I shall be liable to manipulate people in that direction. So the answer of 'being' safeguards the freedom of those for whom I am for as a pastor, and it points in a healthy fashion to the way in which many people often (quite unconsciously and simply because they are naturally 'caring' creatures) fulfil a pastor's role. We are to different people and we can do, individually, to different people, different things. In our desire for explicitness, we should not forget this subtle and delicate and interweaving mechanism of informal pastoral care. Any pretensions to pastoral imperialism are soon dismissed when it is realized just how much effective 'person-to-person' pastoral care goes on within a church congregation, without any intervention from the professional pastor. Indeed, it could be argued (and we shall have more to say about this later) that one of his chief functions is to enable lay-people to exercise more of this informal care.

Over and above this enabling function, there is, however, something else which the minister as pastor must always have (and the secular social-worker may have). It is not so much a claim to uniqueness or distinctiveness, as the challenge to a task. He surely must always, in the words of Cardinal Suhard, Archbishop of Paris in the late forties, seek to 'keep the mystery of God present to man.' It is this which will transfigure his personal life and his pastoral relationships. Suhard went on to say that this meant 'so to live one's life that it would be inexplicable if God did not exist'.[7] Now it might seem as if this is suggesting self-conscious activity, solemnly bringing God and the weight of God's authority to bear on all that the pastor is and does. It is, I believe, nothing of the sort. It is a recognition of a difference of context in the Christian pastoral relationship: namely, that there is an awareness of another dimension, a transcendent reality, which is often lacking in a secular situation of pastoral care, and a conviction that the path to wholeness is not purely of human endeavour and through the interaction of human beings. It is sufficient, however, that that dimension is silently present, without any self-conscious references.

All this suggests that the word which comes nearest to describing the work of the modern pastor is the word 'artist', for the artist always points to a reality beyond himself, and in this case, the mystery of God.

Traditionally, art invites us to contemplate in quietness something whose authority puts us in proper perspective. (One modern view of the artist is, granted, the opposite of this: to invite involvement and participation. Not, that is, to contemplate the drama but to leave my seat in the theatre, rush up on the stage, and take part.) The artist points towards the vision of perfection or wholeness of which he has been made aware, and a glimpse of which he will hope to embody in his work: he will be the agent through whom we may see that which otherwise we might miss. But the true artist will only make a statement, demonstrate, portray; he will not manipulate or persuade. He cannot take away from the viewer the freedom not to see that to which he points, or the freedom to see something quite different from that which the artist sees. A good example of an artist who comes near to giving an entirely fresh view of the fundamentals of human existence is William Blake. 'Life and death, love and hate, good and evil – he perceived these things as directly and freshly as if he had been Adam looking around Eden on the day of his creation . . . Blake asserted that at the age of four he had seen the face of God looking in at the window of his home.'[8] No wonder Blake held the view that the artist is he who communicates the perception of things in their divine essence to other people and points to a divine reality beyond himself.

Now it seems fanciful, even precious, to use the category of the aesthetic to describe the work of the pastor; and it needs further justification. What does it mean 'to keep the mystery of God present to man' and to point to divine reality? To return to the secular social worker: it is not for the Christian, as he is tempted to do, to make judgment as to what motivation sustains him or her in their work. A little experience is sufficient to convince any open-minded person that to divide those of the caring professions into 'Christians and others' on the grounds that the former are more highly-motivated and more richly sustained is an arrogant misreading of the facts. But the explicit task of the minister as pastor is to 'keep the mystery of God present to man'. This does not mean explicit references to him in every pastoral conversation. Indeed, it may precisely be this earnest striving to introduce God which, paradoxically, ensures his seeming absence from that situation. In days when there are so many words of counsel and good advice, it is perhaps only when we stop striving and we wait and look and attend, that the mystery can be present. 'To draw back before the object we are pursuing, only an indirect method is effective. We do nothing if we have not first drawn back. By pulling at the branch, we make all the grapes fall to the ground.'[9]

The keeping of the mystery of God present to man, then, is first a matter of looking, attention. Iris Murdoch, both in her philosophical writings and in her novels, illustrates the way in which 'looking', 'seeing', 'attention' is of crucial importance to a rich, personal life and is an important way of keeping the self in sober perspective. In her philosophical treatise on *The Sovereignty of Good* she describes the way in which art 'affords us a pure delight in the independent existence of what is excellent. Both in its genesis and its enjoyment it is a thing totally opposed to selfish obsession. It invigorates our best faculties and, to use Platonic language, inspires love in the highest part of the soul. It is able to do this partly by virtue of something which it shares with nature: a perfection of form which invites unpossessive contemplation and resists absorption into the selfish dream life of the consciousness.'[10] She describes an experience of nature she has had which illustrates the point: 'I am looking out of my window in an anxious and resentful state of mind, oblivious of my surroundings, brooding perhaps on some damage done to my prestige. Then suddenly I observe a hovering kestrel. In a moment everything is altered. The brooding self with its hurt vanity has disappeared. There is nothing now but kestrel. And when I return to thinking of the other matter it seems less important. And of course this is something which we may also do deliberately: give attention to nature in order to clear our minds of selfish care.'[11] Or, of course, to art: Dora in Iris Murdoch's novel *The Bell* visits the National Gallery and has a similar experience, contemplating the authority of the pictures 'whose presence destroyed the dreary trance-like solipsism of her earlier mood.'[12]

When we truly *see* (a painting, a scene from nature, some object, some person) we afford to the 'other' his proper 'other-ness' and independence: we cease to judge the other, consider its value, simply in relation to *us*. Here, it seems to me, lies hidden just beneath the surface, an incidental wealth of pastoral wisdom: liberation from the pastor's self-concern, self-import-ance, an opportunity to see the other person as he or she truly is. But it is, primarily, an invitation to the pastor to commit himself to *vision*: to the vision of God and the mystery of God. It is to that vision that we must now turn.

2

The Vision of God

The 'vision of God' sounds strange to modern ears. The phrase
has the ring of mediaeval monasticism and abnormal mystical
and ecstatic states. Perhaps the recent re-issue of Kenneth
Kirk's classic work on the subject reflects, or may induce, a
change of atmosphere: at least, it says something about the
persistance of the concept ,even when it has been most neglected.
Kirk was in no doubt as to the centrality of the vision of God in
Christian origins and tradition. 'Christianity had come into the
world with a double purpose, to offer men the vision of God, and
to call them to the pursuit of that vision.'[1] Before the church had
formulated a creed or doctrine of the Trinity, before she had any
fixed liturgical form, or passed any important milestone in her
history, Kirk points out, Irenaeus, the first great post-apostolic
theologian, had declared that 'the glory of God is a living man,
and the life of man is the vision of God'.

Direct biblical evidence for the importance of the phrase is
not strong. Old Testament writers seem to have been unhappy
about the idea if it were thought to relate to an experience in
this life. No man could ever see God and live, and to those
exceptional people like Moses to whom such a vision was
granted, it was only of the 'hinder parts'. In the synoptic gospels,
the reference in the Sermon on the Mount promising the vision
of God to the pure in heart seems to stand by itself and, in any
case, would appear to relate to life beyond death. John is more
explicit. Whilst he is convinced that no man has fully seen God,
that we are simply to look forward to 'see him as he is' (1 John
3.2), God's glory has been seen in his Son, and to see the Son is
also to see the Father. Paul, too, believes that we have already
seen God. 'For the same God who said, "Out of darkness let
light shine", has caused his light to shine within us, to give the

light of revelation – the revelation of the glory of God in the face
of Jesus Christ (II Cor. 4.6). Twice he uses the metaphor of the
mirror (I Cor. 13.13 and II Cor. 3.10) to convey the idea of the
vision of God increasing man's self-knowledge and transforming
him into God's likeness, and like John, he nearly always uses the
word 'we' rather than 'I' in describing vision. He is clear that
any claim to a private visionary experience is not such an
authentic sign of true Christian faith as the quality of love the
Christian displays in his life, the quality at work in a true
Christian community. For both John and Paul, then, the vision
of God is a dominant theme: it is a corporate vision as well as an
individual vision, it is always related to the person of Christ, and
whilst we have glimpses of that vision here, its fruition is only in
the life to come.

To return to the synoptic gospels: it is true that Jesus seems to
have spoken little about seeing God, but as Kirk says, 'He *gave* a
vision of God where others could only *speak* of it.'[2] Whereas
contemporary Judaism largely concentrated on what was
necessary for man to fulfil God's will, Jesus taught of God. He
pictured God at the heart of man's ordinary experience, in
characteristic scenes like children playing in the market-place,
guests at a wedding, farmers sowing in the fields. There the
ordinary becomes the route to the extraordinary, and the place
of surprise is set in the unsurprising place. His unspoken
question in the circumstances always seems to have been, 'Don't
you see?', and this became his spoken question when he
wrestled with his friends' lack of understanding: 'you have eyes:
can you not see?' (Mark 8.17).

Augustine's ideal was the 'vision of God in the city of God'
and he insisted that he had been cornered by the vision, almost
forced to see ('You shone upon me; your radiance enveloped
me; you put my blindness to flight').[3] Nicholas of Cusa in the
fifteenth century, much influenced by Augustine, wrote *The
Vision of God* to help the monks of a Benedictine Abbey focus on
the all-seeing God, as if our vision of God is really the business
of God seeing us:

While I look on this pictured face, whether from the east or
from the west or south, it seemeth in like manner itself to look
on me, and, after the same fashion, according as I move my

face, that face seemeth turned toward me. Even so is Thy face turned toward all faces that look upon Thee. Thy glance, Lord, is Thy face. He, then, who looketh on Thee with loving face will find Thy face looking on himself with love, and the more he shall study to look on Thee with greater love, by so much shall he find Thy face more loving.[4]

Despite these giants of the contemplative life, however, it is not difficult to see why the vision of God came to be regarded by some with suspicion. Extravagant personal testimonies of some mystics conveyed the impression that the vision had already been received, in their private and privileged illumination, and Protestants saw it as another example of justification by works, climbing an individual and rigorous ladder, unaided by God's grace, to reach the vision. This has been reinforced by the exclusive post-Reformation emphasis on the hearing of the gospel, and the absence of the dimension of 'seeing' leads to a distortion of that gospel. 'One of the principal truths of Christianity,' wrote Simone Weil, 'a truth which goes almost unrecognized today, is that the *looking* is what saves us.'[5]

A vignette of the history of communication provides another illustration. In the beginning, man communicated with man visually, through gestures and pictures. The refinement of language and handwritten literature came much later. The advent of the printing-press in the fifteenth century brought the printed word, and five centuries later, wireless brought the broadcast word. But in the late twentieth century, the wheel has come full circle with the development of large-scale technological visual-aids and television. It is significant that Christians are 'innocents abroad' in the field of religious television. It is as if we have hardly begun to know how to communicate visually, and that is tragic for a faith whose founder 'opened the eyes of the blind' to the God who was always present in the midst of the ordinary world. So we are left with programmes like *Stars on Sunday* or attempts through television to communicate concepts and ideas by means of talking heads, and as Kenneth Clark realized when preparing his *Civilization* series, television is a poor medium in this respect. He found himself in difficulty, he said, with regard to law and philosophy, because he could not think of any way of making them visually interesting. It is surely because we have so conceptualized Christian faith, and forgotten that it is primarily an invitation to see, that we are as yet so inadequate at producing programmes of worth and quality. (The blame is often put on low budgets: it really lies in the lack of sufficient theological artists to furnish us with telling contemporary parables.)

Perhaps the modern theologian who has most called attention to the primacy of vision, the necessity to see, is Ian Ramsey. He liked to take A. N. Whitehead's description of religion as his starting-point: 'Religion is the vision of something which stands beyond, behind, and within, the passing flux of immediate things, something which is real, and yet waiting to be realized; something which is a remote possibility, and yet the greatest of present facts; something that gives meaning to all that passes and yet eludes apprehension; something whose possession is the final good, and yet is beyond all reach; something which is the ultimate ideal and the hopeless quest.' Without that vision, human life is a 'bagatelle of transient experience'.[6] Now, Ramsey argued, it is when that human experience takes on an extra dimension and depth which we perceive, when there occurs what he calls a 'cosmic disclosure' that we can rightly use the word 'religious'. A favourite expression of his was 'when the penny drops', or in other words, 'when I see'. He illustrated the importance of 'seeing' in this sense from John's account of the two disciples going to the tomb on Easter morning.[7] John, stooping and looking in, 'seeth the linen clothes lying' – and the Greek verb used simply denotes the act of turning the head in a particular direction in good light, and keeping the eyes open. Peter 'beholdeth the linen clothes lying, and the napkin that was upon his head not lying with the linen clothes but rolled up in a place by itself' – and the Greek verb now used is one which denotes looking with an eye to detail. But 'then entered in the other disciple also, which came first to the tomb, and he saw and believed', and yet a third different Greek verb is used which includes physical 'seeing', but goes far beyond it to discernment, a response to a disclosure: it is as if something breaks in on us, and the 'penny drops'.

Another favourite expression of Ian Ramsey's was 'and more'. The vision of the eternal is disclosed to us through the temporal: it relates to what is seen – *and more*. And we gain access to this 'more' not by trying to peer into another and supernatural realm, but by being awakened to it, by coming to see. It becomes a matter of widening our horizons, or as Blake might have said, 'cleansing the doors of our perception' – even in a fish-and-chip shop. Ramsey liked to quote the example of Charles Raven walking back from Liverpool Cathedral one winter evening at the time of the early thirties' depression in Lancashire, and passing a crowded fish-and-chip shop. The over-familiar sight of the shop, the ritual of scooping out the chips and emptying them on to the greaseproof and the news-paper needs no detailing: but of that customary scene, Raven wrote, 'All of a sudden, the *glory* . . .' The ordinary became the extraordinary: the proprietor symbolized in that context the heavenly Father giving his children their daily bread.

This has implications for persons, for educators and for the church. Beyond any description of personality that natural and behavioural sciences may yield, the man who is saved, made whole, is the man who responds to a vision of God's life in Christ. We become aware of what Ramsey calls our 'transcendent subjectivity' as we affirm ourselves in some situation or dis-closure; we are 'characteristically ourselves' when we acknow-ledge the authority of the vision of a moral obligation. The implication for educators is that their task is not to hand out information, nor to try to indoctrinate those whom they teach, but to provide the atmosphere and climate where disclosure-situations might more easily occur. 'Theology is the pioneering of a vision, and in so far as we give any meaning to a phrase like "theology of education" then the structure of the school com-munity – staff/pupil relations, character of the teaching – must reflect a common exploration. It must reflect the images of the pioneer and lover, rather than be made up of communities where one person retails to many what he considers to be universal truth.'[8] For the church, likewise, Ramsey saw that if it does not find ways and means of opening up moments of vision and disclosure, there will be no 'cash value' to be given to anything it says or does. We need above all to make possible occasions when society can rediscover some sense of the sublime.

We do not give a lead – though those who ask us for one often suppose we do – by reiterating conclusions which those around us wish to hear or wish to have without the trouble of reaching them. We give a lead only by displaying, in our utterances or otherwise, that which inspires us. 'The power of God is the worship he inspires', said Whitehead. The implication is sometimes that the only food suited to the sheep, and the only food they desire, is a prescribed diet of food devoid of roughage: which a moment's reflection will tell us is entirely unhealthy.[9]

This philosophy of 'and more', this emphasis on vision and seeing as being integral to and derivative of Christian faith, is far removed in spirit from more conventional notions of 'getting the message across', or from the concept of Christianity as a set of propositions to be heard or read and learnt and then used as the basis of deductions about life and morals. It is far removed, too, from the struggle which has gone on for so long in this century to establish some *relevance* of God in a secular age. God is not to be fitted in: he is to be discovered, pursued. Perhaps it was never better (if surprisingly) expressed than in the Report of the Carlisle Commission, *Partners in Education*: 'God's revealing manner is not authoritarian' . . . and 'the theology arising from such a revelation is therefore seen to be not as a body of eternal final truths to be reached down and "put across". It is rather a summons, urgent but not coercive, to see more and see it more profoundly, to know more and know it better, to love more and love more richly. It is to realize that the truth is not something which we have for our own possession and to our own prescription, but a life into which we grow.'[10] So just as the parables of Jesus were an invitation to his hearers to see a God-ward dimension in events as commonplace as a woman baking bread or sweeping out a room, so Christian faith becomes an invitation to see what others see and have seen in Jesus Christ.

Whence, then, comes the stimulation to vision? Two obvious sources readily spring to mind: the Bible and the liturgy. No one surely would be so foolish as to deny the way in which a reading of the Bible can stretch horizons, or the way its self-authenticating passages (e.g. Ps. 23, Isa. 53, I Cor. 13, Rom. 8) have awakened and inspired and sustained many faithful Christians. We depend on the Bible to 'check' our vision of Christ which is such a crucial stimulus to growth. The remarkable success of Alec McCowen's recent reading of the gospel according to St Mark in a London theatre and on the television screen reminded me that it was a solitary reading of the Passion narrative in St Mark one Good Friday that proved formative for me in adolescence and led to a situation of disclosure Perhaps we need equally to recognize that the Bible can blur vision, and indeed sometimes encourage myopia. It is a useful servant, but a very bad master: or to change the metaphor, it is to be seen as a spring-board, and not as a bed. Ever since the Reformation, historical realism seems to have killed the symbolic and figurative interpretation of the Bible that was prevalent in the mediaeval era, and the extension of literacy has led to greater literalism which restricts rather than enlarges vision. We need a reawakening of the poetic imagination over vast stretches of our culture if the Bible is ever again to speak properly to us. Further, pastoral injunctions to read the Bible have created over-confident expectations of what the Bible can (or should even try to) achieve – or a paralysing sense of guilt, since it is always presented as a *sine qua non* of Christian faith. The position is not made easier by the zeal of those sects, the members of whom (it is said) 'know their Bible backwards' . . . But to rely on the Bible to solve dilemmas, to believe that Bible reading *must* be a 'spiritual exercise' is to have the eyes focussed down rather than upwards towards the vision of God. It can foster a spirit of dependence rather than lead towards maturity. The Bible is not a programme, or a training manual. As soon as it is realized how the gospels came to be written, what sort of source-material they are, a series of halting hints and glimpses which the different authors had of Jesus, they can only be used as an invitation to vision. The point of reading the Bible is to relive that disclosure of God which the Bible story is depicting, and then use it to stimulate the imagination to see his disclosure in the contemporary scene. The biblical 'facts' that a mature Christian need know are few. Detailed knowledge of the temple architecture, or of what happens when a man removes his neighbour's landmark, or the ability to draw illuminated sketch-maps of Paul's journeys may be of historical interest and absorbing to some: none of it is necessarily significant for the Christian on the road to maturity. A course for laymen (on 'The

limitations of the Bible'?) could much more profitably bury that
prevalent and wistful notion that mere assimilation of biblical
facts will of itself produce that personal vision and insight which
is essential. 'Before the Bible can speak to us and tell us anything,
before we can teach the Bible to others, we must break down
any idolatry of descriptive language; we must create sensitivity
and foster the imagination.'[11]

Even those parts of the Bible which directly relate to vision
can be wrongly and prescriptively interpreted. Isaiah's vision in
the temple (Isa. 6) is such a case. There is a neat progression as
Isaiah describes that vision from the adoration of the 'Lord, high
and lifted up' to the realization of the prophet's unworthiness –
'a man of unclean lips' – to the commission to service – 'Here
am I, send me' – a pattern which has been woven in a thousand
pulpits. It is a pattern that bears all the marks of naturalness
and authenticity. But the implication to be resisted is that which
suggests that every vision of God must follow that pattern.
Admittedly, it may be difficult for me to see how any true vision
will fail to convince me of my inadequacy or fail to make me
wish to 'follow the star'; but my vision may simply inspire in me
a sense of gratitude and a longing to be. It may, in other words,
simply promote in me aspiration and pursuit of the vision rather
than any definite conviction. But because this is *my* vision, it is
to this that I must hold rather than believe that it is inferior
because it does not correspond to the form which the prophet
Isaiah's took. To press every vision into the strait-jacket of one
pattern is, in the end, to lose vision, and that is the danger of
using every incident in the Bible as a final touchstone.

The other obvious resource of vision is liturgy, since clearly it
was originally intended to articulate the vision of God-in-Christ
and recreate it week by week for those who participate in it. In
experience, various factors seem to combine to defeat that
recreation. The sameness of the service makes for a mechanical
and over-formalized atmosphere; the nature of 'sacramental
grace' gives the impression of a weekly topping-up process; the
backward-looking nature of much liturgy (heavy scripture
readings, the being taken back to the Upper Room) suggests
ossification rather than a road to vision. And all this has little
to do with the question as to whether the liturgy is framed in
traditional language or is revised and in modern speech. 'It is

perhaps significant that the new forms have failed to bring as much fresh vitality to the worship of existing congregations as might have been hoped,' writes the Dean of Worcester. 'For the most part people do not *enjoy* going to church as much as once they did. Do I? Do you? Some magic seems to have departed.'[12] It is a gloomy conclusion, but with our present liturgical arrangements, perhaps it is inevitable, and the addition of a few guitars, some speaking in tongues and coffee at the back of the church afterwards are only going to hide the real problem still further. We are paying dearly for our massive concentration on liturgical change. At that point where the Liturgical Movement has had its greatest success in encouraging frequent lay communions, the act itself has been impoverished because of insufficient attention to more 'interior' matters of preparation and a proper devotion. Now that an *ex opere operato* view of the sacrament has largely been abandoned, a greater responsibility is placed on the worshipper 'to get out of the liturgy what you put into it'. Sometimes, however depressing or even damnable one's present mood, the liturgy does seem to 'take off', but the need for preparation and a proper devotion was never more vital. And of the reformed liturgies, inspired by the Movement, could it not generally be said that it is the *and more* which is largely missing? Homeliness, even familiarity, abound; it is the extra dimensions of disclosure and depth which often seem missing, and they arise, not as a result of self-conscious effort to produce feelings of the 'numinous' and 'mystery', but as a result of personal or corporate awareness.

Perhaps part, at least, of our problem is that we do things the wrong way round. We need our vision first, the vision that emerges from a shared experience of genuine human living and community, and then we will try to give liturgical shape to the vision, however simple. Some of the acts of worship I have experienced lately which have most come alive for me have been those when I have shared as tutor in a religious studies weekend with adult students of varying degrees and kinds of faith – and sometimes of none. By the time Sunday morning arrives, the general will seems to be that, because we have shared as a group richly and honestly, we should 'have a service' in which this could be articulated. The service is short and participatory and very often includes more silence than

words. But the shared life is the secret: real experience is set
within a liturgical framework. Merely to provide that framework and hope that the experience will necessarily ensue may be
a vain delusion.

Even this superficial exploration of Bible and liturgy indicates
that we cannot pin our hopes on these two sources alone for the
nurturing and sustaining of vision. Indeed, too much reliance on
them can possibly deflect us from true pastoral aims. We need a
more radical exploration.

3

Vision and Growth

Few people who visit Cape Canaveral in Florida are likely to miss the significant part which vision plays in man's achievements. 'Progress is the growth of vision';[1] space-travel is an excellent example of a vision so capturing man's imagination that eventually it becomes practical politics. Perhaps it also illustrates the way in which, when this earth affords us no more deserts to cross, or continents to explore, our need for vision prompts us to jump off the well-known limitations of terrestrial space into an unknown spatial sphere. Patrick Moore relates how when he was in his teens he attended a scientific meeting in London, and presented a paper concerning observations he had been making of the moon. He made a confident prediction that man would land on the moon before AD 2000. 'These schoolboys have wild ideas,' someone remarked: and yet, of course, Patrick Moore was needlessly pessimistic in his forecast by more than thirty years. Not only has the target been reached: we have become bored by the subject. It has taken us less than twenty years to change from being sceptical and slightly amused at the prospect to this feeling of boredom with the achievement. Space-travel has had the paradoxical effect of making us rather fearful and parochial. As Dotty remarks in Tom Stoppard's play, *Jumpers*, 'Man is on the moon, his feet on solid ground, and he has seen us whole, all in one go, *little* – local . . .'[2] A vision achieved is a vision in dissolution; or, as the schoolboy essay from Robert L. Stevenson prosaically expresses it, 'to travel hopefully is better than to arrive'.

The notion of vision as the spur to achievement in the scientific world may be a cliché. Similarly it has become commonplace to point to the notion of the journey, the pilgrim's progress towards the vision of God which lies at the heart of the

Christian tradition: not just in the writings of the mystics, but in witnesses as different as George Herbert and Charles Kingsley. But in pastoral teaching and guidance, the concept of vision does not necessarily find support as quickly as the tradition might indicate. For many of us the concept of vision is too long-term. We are like those who visit doctors and counsellors and expect a quick resolution of their problems, the 'magic wand' touch. It is also too vague. That which is indirect, and oblique – perceived here, missed there – does not offer the sort of flat, incontrovertible (but attractive) certainty which is desired. It demands the cultivation of those virtues of perception and patience which are quiet and undramatic. (How near we often get to demanding that faith becomes sight, rather than insight! We need, in this sense, to put a lot of question marks around the Shroud of Turin.) You cannot by vision storm people into the Kingdom of God: vision does not easily allow for any precise division between the haves and the have-nots, the saved and the unsaved. It is fitful, not regular or systematic. It will not necessarily answer the call of earnest prayer or even rigorous discipline. It is of the essence of vision that one fleeting glimpse draws you to the next, one staging-post to the next – but with no prospect of exhausting the vision in this life. If it did, we might be as blasé about it as we are now about space-travel. Further, although it appears at first sight to be a contradiction, vision requires what seems like hard work on the part of those who see. We need to act on vision before it turns sour and destructive. There is the difficulty each time of leaving home, going out into the unknown in Abrahamic fashion, in response to the vision – and it all feels threatening and dangerous. I sometimes feel that the weakness of the church at present is not so much its lack of vision, as its pusillanimity in not acting on insights long ago reached. This is a failure which ultimately kills the vision itself with guilt and shame and the rationalization of cowardice. And the corresponding, exciting truth is that vision acted upon leads into further vision.

Progress towards vision and journeying towards a goal: if the pastor is an artist pointing towards the mystery of God, he will be concerned with that progress and journeying. He will see himself as an enabler of vision, and hence of personal growth. What is perhaps surprising, and certainly tragic, is that such growth is heard of more in secular than in Christian circles.

Concerns of the institution – the ordination of women, the politicization of the church – and its very survival loom large in the current Christian scene; little is made of the quiet but crucial dimension of growth and sanctification. The impression often given is that once you have made the difficult decision of faith and become a member of the Body of Christ, nothing important remains to be done except perhaps to keep faithfully where you are, and above all, not to 'be missing'. The traditional notion that you are *going* somewhere, on a journey of growth and exploration, seems to have been lost. Paul knew that in spite of being converted and justified, something else remained: 'Forgetting what is behind me, and reaching out for that which lies ahead, I press towards the goal to win the prize which is God's call to the life above, in Christ Jesus' (Phil. 3.13). John's first letter looks forward and says that 'what we shall be has not yet been disclosed, but we know that when it is disclosed, we shall be like him, because we shall see him as he is. Everyone who has this hope before him purifies himself, as Christ is pure' (I John 3.2). This necessity for sanctification, for growth towards the vision of God, is an emphasis we badly need to recall. The quality of our Christian living is not given its proper due. Obviously, the Holy Spirit is the agent of sanctification: but human beings often seem to be used as instruments of the Spirit, and in this case, to be means of growth in and for other people. This is especially true of pastors, who against all those pressures of modern life which would reduce man to a number or a pre-determined mechanism, stand up for the high dignity of man, his potentiality and his destiny. Had Paul's picture of 'mature manhood, measured by nothing less than the full stature of Christ' been afforded its proper priority in the life of the church and the pastoral ministry, the story of contemporary Christian faith might be very different.

Meanwhile, the Personal Growth Movement, inspired by humanist psychologists and psychotherapists, flourishes. The early apostle of the Movement, Carl Rogers, rejects the medical model as a proper model for coping with people's personal and psychological problems and prefers to focus on that potential we all possess for growth and development which it is possible to release, given the right psychological climate. Human beings,

it is argued, have legitimate goals *as* human beings: the psycho-
therapist Anthony Storr says that it is 'unscientific' to omit
mention of goals in describing human behaviour, and the
humanistic psychologist Abraham Maslow calls the process
of 'self-actualization' (or 'maturity') 'the goal of human
striving'. All three give us the impression of living as the
continuous unfolding of unrealized potential. More interesting
still: there seems to be some consensus amongst those in the
psychological field, however independently they worked, concerning the characteristics such self-actualized or mature people
will display. They will be, for instance, accepting, spontaneous,
able to enjoy privacy, 'peak-experiences', and humour, and to
relate to others irrespective of race, class, education or religion,
having some few relationships which are able to go deep. C. G.
Jung in his description of a similar 'way of individuation' in his
book *Integration of the Personality* speaks of the way in which life
offers to us certain conventions – moral, social, religious and
political, and for most people, these conventions represent some
secure resting-places. They are 'a flight from the final consequence of one's own being' and accommodate rather well those
who fear going further along the road to wholeness. But those
who are 'historical personalities' owe their growth not to their
'unconditional subjection *to* convention' but to their 'liberating
freedom *from* convention'. 'They thrust themselves up like
mountain peaks out of the mass that clung to its collective fears,
convictions, laws and methods, and choose their own way. And
to the ordinary human being it always seemed wonderful that
someone should prefer to the beaten track, with its known
destination, a small steep path that leads to the unknown.'[3]

There are other secular witnesses to the importance of
personal maturity. In the preface to his play, *A Man for All
Seasons*, Robert Bolt says that it is the gift of mature selfhood
which he sees as the paramount gift our thinkers, artists and
men of science should try to foster. He deplores the fact that we
no longer have 'any picture of individual Man by which to
recognize ourselves and against which to measure ourselves'.
He apologizes for the fact that since he is not a Catholic or in any
meaningful sense of the word, a Christian, he finds what he
calls such a 'hero of selfhood' in a man like Thomas More,
designated a Christian saint. It is as if he had never expected to

find maturity and sanctity so closely allied. 'What first attracted me was a person who could not be accused of any incapacity for life, who indeed seized life in great variety and almost greedy quantities, who nevertheless found something in himself without which life was valueless and when that was denied him was able to grasp his death.'[4]

These descriptions of those who are on the road to maturity may well bring to mind a portrait of the Man, Jesus Christ. Here is a portrait painted by Harry Williams:

> We find a Christ who was not a saint as that term is commonly and mistakenly understood. We find a Christ who did not always do the ideal thing. We discover that the notion that He did is wishful thinking – a refusal to accept the full fact of His humanity. For in human life, it is generally not possible to do the ideal thing. The claims men have to meet very often clash with each other, so that you cannot give to every claim what is its due. So, for instance, Jesus gave Himself to His work at the expense of His family to whom He appears to have been brutal. And Jewish scholars of great integrity have noticed that Jesus was so concerned to proclaim His own message that He was sometimes unfair to His opponents. In the circumstances of human life that sort of one-sidedness is inevitable. And Jesus was not magically preserved from the contradictions, the conflicting claims which are the inevitable lot of men. But in one thing He was absolutely consistent. The truth He proclaimed, the truth by which He lived, the truth for which He died, was His own. He discovered it for Himself within Himself. He did not buy it ready-made from its professional purveyors. On that point He never compromised. That is why the people heard Him with astonishment and recognized that He taught with authority and not as the scribes. He spoke, that is from His own first-hand experience and not from an acquired knowledge of other people's ideas. He did not mould His person or His ministry to any pre-conceived notion. He carefully avoided the application to Himself of any title which might suggest such pre-conceptions. If he applied passages of the Old Testament to Himself, we do not know which ones He selected. Was it Isaiah? Was it Daniel? Was it both? Was it neither? This

uncompromising loyalty to His own identity, to the truth which was Himself, brought Him power and joy . . . But He had also to pay the price which must always be paid by those who have the courage to receive their own vision instead of accepting the available stereotypes – isolation, loneliness, the ultimate opposition of the crowds.[5]

It is obvious from this description and from that of the humanistic psychologists that we are not here in a world of perfection or halo-conferring. The mature person is not the 'ideal person', the one who from a particular moral standpoint has reached perfection. The gospel injunction, 'Be ye perfect', which has caused such feelings of guilt and inadequacy in so many people should really be translated, 'be rounded, complete, mature': and maturity cannot be seen as a fixed, predictable goal or static point. Rather it is a road, a direction of movement. 'Each growth stage has its new opportunities and hazards, with fresh frustrations and unexpected open doors. Whatever else the future is, it is always a surprise.'[6] It is important to recognize that maturity and moral perfection are not synonymous, since any fullness of vision will have to include the dark side of our being, the almost cosmic battle that we all know within ourselves, even when we find it hard to admit it. Christian faith has somehow found it harder to integrate this truth than, for instance, Hinduism, where the double identity of divinity has within it both creator and destroyer. This failure to deal with the dark forces, except as identifiable sins against some ethical code, has vitiated much Christian teaching, and made the lives of some Christians more miserable than necessary. It has also made very unreal the notion of the 'saint', and persuaded us that we need to take some unusual and heroic road to win the prize of perfection in the end. (Is this why the church has often presented saints as people not conditioned by the same physical and psychological forces which operate on the rest of us?) We need to see sanctity above all as 'ordinary, that is ordinariness so much loved and treasured, so much polished and cherished, that it becomes extraordinary.'[7] It is significant that Monica Furlong uses here the same terminology of ordinary/extraordinary as that used by Ian Ramsey to describe what happens when the dimension of faith or transcendency pierces our ordinary experience and the disclosure given makes the experience extraordinary, needing a strange poetic language in order properly to describe it.

There is, then, a certain correspondence between the psychological goal of maturity and the Christian goal of sanctification. Perhaps Bonhoeffer summed it up when he said that our goal is 'to be a man, pure and simple, as Jesus was a man': and such a genuine human being will be one of us, not fenced off from us in some small holy huddle. There is an interesting conversation in *The Plague*, the novel by the atheist Albert Camus, between Tarrou who organizes sanitary squads to cope with the plague and the doctor, Rieux. It is a summer evening, and they are sitting on the terrace, sniffing the sea air and listening to the rattle of the ambulances. 'What interests me,' Tarrou says, 'is learning how to become a saint.' 'But you don't believe in God.' 'Exactly. Can one be a saint without God? – that's the problem, in fact the only problem, I'm up against today.' . . . 'Perhaps,' the doctor answered. 'But, you know, I feel more fellowship with the defeated than with saints. Heroism and sanctity don't really appeal to me, I imagine. What interests me is – being a man.'[8]

Nevertheless, despite this common insistence on 'being a man', there is an important divide between Christian and psychological conceptions, and certainly, on how we achieve such maturity of manhood. Paul C. Vitz, associate Professor of Psychology at New York University, has recently written a powerful (almost emotional) attack on *Psychology as Religion: the cult of self-worship*. He puts his finger on the difference between the two approaches: within psychology, 'the relentless and single-minded search for and glorification of the self is at direct cross-purposes with the Christian injunction to lose the self.' 'What is excluded is the spiritual life of prayer, meditation and worship – the essential vertical dimension of Christianity, the relation to God. Selfism is an example of a horizontal heresy, with its emphasis only on the present, and on self-centred ethics. At its very best (which is not often) it is Christianity without the first commandment.'[9] In so far as the goal is *my* maturity, *my* self-actualization, and nothing necessarily beyond, that is a just criticism, but to be fair to Abraham Maslow, who coined the term 'self-actualization', such a person will be orientated to things outside himself, to a mission in life. Interestingly, too, Robert Bolt suggests that a clear sense of the self can only crystallize round something transcendental. The Christian will be concerned about his own growth – but also, and paradoxically, unconcerned: concerned that his growth towards the embodiment of Christ's love and life takes place, unconcerned in that so long as he places the emphasis on his growth, that growth is unlikely to happen. The idea that the Christian should all the time be taking his own spiritual temperature is surely false. 'Is there a man of you who by anxious thought can add a foot to his height?' (Matt. 6.27). The Christian does not happen to be looking at himself: he is taken up by the vision of God-in-Christ, and the measure of his responses to that vision will be the measure of his growth. It will be the journey to that vision which he will find himself taking, and his relationship with his Father, where his life is hidden with Christ-in-God in prayer and sacrament, will sustain him on the journey. Unlike the psychological model, the Christian will not be trying to make something of himself. Set in the context of the vision of God, unselfconscious humility and a refusal to take himself solemnly or pompously will be his distinctive characteristic.

I find it most encouraging to see the way in which Iris Murdoch, as a humanist philosopher, sees so clearly the relationship between 'vision' and 'goodness'. 'Any religion or ideology', she writes, 'can be degraded by the substitution of self, usually in some disguise, for the true object of veneration.' That is why she thinks

> there is a place both inside and outside religion for a sort of contemplation of the Good, not just by dedicated experts but by ordinary people: an attention which is not just the planning of particular good actions but an attempt to look right away from self towards a distant transcendent perfection, a source of uncontaminated energy, a source of *new* and quite undreamt-of virtue.[10]

Our 'background condition' must be a 'just mode of vision', and when it is, the 'rare virtue' of humility will be the result. 'Only rarely does one meet somebody in whom it positively shines, in whom one apprehends with amazement the absence of the anxious avaricious tentacles of the self . . . The humble man, because he sees himself as nothing, can see other things as they are.'[11] Where is there a more moving picture of the inwardness of Christian life, and its effect?

It is the privilege of the pastor to present this 'just mode of vision' through his portrayal of Jesus as the lure and attraction to growth and sanctification. And how much more compelling than the oft-quoted but quite unrealistic 'imitation of Christ'! At present, he has, as they say, a lot going for him. The contemporary fascination with the person of Jesus expressed in some films, musicals, folk-music and off-beat poetry is in stark contrast to the general boredom and irritation with the institutional church. To pursue such a vision means that we shall not be dictated to by literalism or constrained by legalistic detail. We shall not be anxious about the effects of gospel criticism or our lack of certainty in what we know about the earthly life of Jesus; we shall find room for spontaneity in following him; we shall not succumb, in any sense of spiritual pride, to the feeling that we have 'arrived'. And if it be objected that our portrait is a subjective portrait, we shall accept the criticism as just and inevitable; but not wholly so. We do have some standard of reference in the gospels.

This means, in turn, that we shall not see the moral and good character as he who simply takes right decisions and makes wise judgments. Recent Christian ethics has perhaps concentrated too hard on decision and action, and not enough on the attempt to clarify vision, and this merely feeds the ingrained heresy that Christian living is simply and negatively 'not doing anything wrong'. The moral life is primarily one of 'attention', in Simone Weil's word, rather than of will: 'the love which brings the right answer' in complex moral questions 'is an exercise of justice and realism and really looking', as Iris Murdoch says, for the difficulty is always to keep the attention fixed on the real situation, and stop it from sliding back to the self in self-pity or resentment, fantasy or despair. And when the Christian life is understood as the life of attention or looking, then every day and the details of every day begin to matter more profoundly. Christian concern with 'ethical issues' often gives the impression that Christian life has no business or relationship with the ordinary routine of life, which might seem morally uninteresting. But it is in the midst of that routine, not in the 'big issues' or 'significant events', that the Christian vision is tested, and a true perspective developed.

The more man goes out from himself or goes beyond himself, the more the spiritual dimension of his life is deepened, the more he becomes truly man, the more also he grows in likeness to God, who is Spirit. On the other hand, the more he turns inward and encloses himself in self-interest, the less human does he become. This is the strange paradox of spiritual being – that precisely by going out and spending itself, it realizes itself.[12]

The curse of the contemporary emphasis on personal growth is its narcissism: the secret of sanctification is the abandonment of every attempt to cultivate the self, or in a still simpler formula, coming from the heart of the gospel, it is losing oneself to find oneself.

4

Awareness and Self-Awareness

There are few words more misused than 'spirituality'. To many, it suggests a private, pious state of preoccupation with one's own inner condition which, as we have seen, is not the road to sanctification. Fundamentally, as John Macquarrie argues, spirituality has to do with 'becoming a person in the fullest sense':[1] this does justice both to the Christian tradition which sees in Jesus the pattern for all humanity and to the contemporary concern with the conditions necessary for human life to reach its fulfilment. Now I have already argued that seeing, looking, lie at the heart of Christian faith and life: I want now to develop that theme a little more, and suggest that awareness is an important mark of the mature person, lies at the heart of spirituality, and lays upon the pastor the task of 'opening the eyes of the blind' and awakening the imagination.

'The place from which all spirituality must *begin*, that is,' is 'the created world around us,' wrote Ian Ramsey.[2] Perhaps no modern theologian or thinker better illustrates this truth than Pierre Teilhard de Chardin. He devotes the foreword in his work, *The Phenomenon of Man*, to 'seeing'.

We might say that the whole of life lies in that verb – if not ultimately, at least essentially . . . The history of the living world can be summarized as the elaboration of ever more perfect eyes within a cosmos in which there is always something more to be seen. After all, do we not judge the perfection of an animal, or the supremacy of a thinking being, by the penetration and synthetic power of their gaze? To try to see more and better is not a matter of whim or curiosity or self-indulgence. *To see or to perish* is the very condition laid upon everything that makes up the universe, by means of the mysterious gift of existence. And this, in superior measure, is man's condition.[3]

It was Teilhard's early passion for rocks and stones which led him to the conviction that 'the perception of the divine omnipresence is essentially a seeing, a taste, that is to say a sort of intuition bearing upon certain superior qualities in things'.[4] His natural observations enabled him to see a universe on fire with divine love, betraying a presence which lures and embraces man; a world in all its manifold aspects united with God. So, too, John Stewart Collis, scientist, philosopher and man of religion, says that he sees ordinary things as if they had never been seen before. He starts from the scientific facts about the created order. Facts, he says, are his chief stimulus 'because they heighten my sense of significance. My pursuit of facts is for the sake of imagination. I always want to relate my physics with metaphysics.'[5] All this is to suggest that spirituality is a matter not of striving after another world, but having a deepened awareness of this world.

How then does the pastor 'open the eyes of the blind'? I have found as a result of trying to help some people who recognize the validity of prayer but seem imprisoned in their own deadness that simple contemplative and wordless exercises can stimulate new life. The business of being still and looking at a natural object – it may be a flower, a plant, a picture – for five to ten minutes, can help the deliberate cultivation of the seeing eye, and openness to different forms, shapes and colours. This is not to be caught in some narrow aesthetic strait-jacket, where only beauty and nature go together. Perhaps the length of time that elapsed before L. S. Lowry was recognized as a painter has something to do with the traditional assumption that the dark satanic hills of industrialism were the very antithesis of beauty. In catching and reproducing a dimension in a Salford slum that nearly everyone else had missed, the painter opened the eyes of the blind. In the nineteenth century, it was Fr Dolling's great aim through the provision he made for the senses in the worship of his church in the slums of Portsmouth to put the drab lives of his congregation in a rich, life-affirming context. Those who live in and on the outskirts of industrial cities today are most in need not of large church buildings, but of small oases where in quiet they can contemplate one or two objects of beauty amidst the brashness and tawdriness all around them. Even more, they need to be able to look at those lines, perspectives and exquisite details which still exist, and which to the seeing eye have not been swamped by the squalor. It has become fashionable to set in opposition care for buildings and care for people: there are occasions when care for buildings and what goes inside them betrays considerable pastoral care.

The pastor, therefore, helps to stimulate awareness not through elaborate and exotic techniques, but by furthering people's capacity to see in the given circumstances of their lives. It will be a matter of making contact with people where they are and building on what glimpses they already have of the mystery of life, helping them to see a dimension and depth they would otherwise miss. And *people* they would otherwise miss, too. Compared with that of other religious reformers, the ministry of Jesus appears to have an air of casualness about it. He did not try to promote any new system of law or formulate plans for a new and better world order. No new view of society emerges from his teaching: hence, the endless arguments of social theologians about Christian social teaching. What he did seems to have been devastatingly simple: in the words of Helmut Thielicke, he 'makes us see anew the blind man there at the corner, the prostitute in her self-despising, the rich young ruler with his inner emptiness, the old woman in her loneliness. He only shows us the human being next to us.'[6] The person who never notices the person next to him can never move beyond and see the 'incognito' Christ in him. Busyness can lead pastors to miss seeing those they meet: people can be a hindrance in a carefully-planned schedule for the day, since they are so unpredictable and time-consuming. And simply to be noticed, recognized as a person, transforms the day for many people. In this, church pastors are especially at risk, for they may unconsciously make a distinction between those 'inside' and those 'outside' the church. They may notice the Christians, and miss the human beings. Simone Weil's refusal to be baptized, in spite of her great sympathy for and love of the Catholic faith and liturgy, has often been remarked upon. She thought that belonging to a body of people who called themselves 'we' would mean she would no longer be able to move among men of every class and complexion, mixing with them and sharing their life and outlook, so far that is to say as conscience allows, merging into the crowd and disappearing among them, so that they show themselves as they are, putting off all disguises with me. It is because I long to know them, so as to love them just as they are. For if I do not love them as they are, it will not be they whom I love, and my love will be unreal.[7]

Despite corporate loyalties and the necessity for a Christian community called the church, we should always be sensitive to this tension in which we are involved, a tension perhaps to which only something of the capacity to see as Jesus saw can keep us alerted.

In stimulating awareness and encouraging to wider horizons 'truth through fiction' can be useful. Modern novels and drama are often superficially dismissed in a pastoral context as being risky to faith and morals. My experience is that they can open the eyes even of those unversed in literature, as they portray in flesh-and-blood form those questions which disturb people and cause them such agonizing. We must not search for confirmation of faith through modern literature: it is simply that our power to see will be strengthened, our sympathies widened, our ability to identify with others enriched. Surely no one can read the first novel Albert Camus wrote, *The Outsider*,[8] without understanding better the way in which the authenticity of our lives is spoilt by convention and so-called 'tact': nor his last novel, *The Fall*,[9] without realizing more fully the insidious nature of guilt and its effect on human beings. The novels of William Golding, Saul Bellow and others (the list is considerable) all illuminate what it is like to be alive in the twentieth century. The setting-up of a group to study David Anderson's Christian survey of some modern literature, *The Tragic Protest*,[10] and the novels discussed might be a brave pastoral exercise for some. It would certainly produce many uncomfortable moments for the leader and some of the members, but it would be a stretching of the imagination and opening of the eyes, not to mention a facing of some hard truths.

Modern drama will yield similar examples. Those who study Graham Greene's first play, *The Living Room*, must surely always remain suspicious in the future of religious slogans and catch-phrases, a besetting temptation for Christians. Take, for instance, the passage towards the end of the play in which Rose Pemberton, desperate in her fight for her love of a married man against the conventions of a church and society in which she has been nurtured, is in conversation with her uncle James, a Catholic priest. 'I just want a bit of ordinary human comfort. Not formulas. "Love God. Trust God. Everything will be alright one day." Uncle, please say something that's not Catholic.'[11] (And Catholic, of course, means nothing more than doctrinally orthodox or sound. Had Rose been of another persuasion, the word *Protestant* would have been equally valid.) And when Rose is finally driven to the brink of suicide because of the state of moral confusion in which she finds herself, her uncle – trying hard to leap over the gulf which separates his cool orthodoxies from her passionate experience of life – confesses that all he has to offer is 'the Penny Catechism'. 'There's always the Mass,' he says. 'There's your Rosary . . . Perhaps Our lady,' and then in one final fling of despair – 'Prayer.'[12] But Uncle James does not need convincing of the barrenness of his own case: and the sleeping-tablets lie too close to Rose's hands.

Another and less obvious example might be Harold Pinter. His name is popularly associated with banality and obscurity: but anyone who perseveres with his plays begins to see 'ordinary and everyday events which he had not before noticed with such intensity of insight that they transcend themselves and become symbolic of a whole category of experience'.[13] Pinter has 'created his own personal world in his own personal idiom, wholly consistent, wholly individual, an expression of his own anguish, peopled from *his* wound which yet, as great poetry always does, re-echoes in the depths of the minds of a multitude of individuals and is capable of giving voice to unspoken fears, sufferings and yearnings shared by all mankind.'[14] Is there not here sufficient stimulus to human awareness, a call to a larger vision?

Awareness implies self-awareness, that I shall see not only other people, but also myself with my strengths and weaknesses, without falling into the error of either taking myself too solemnly or considering myself valueless. If I am unaware, I will never allow myself to come to terms with what lies below the level of my consciousness: my darker side will dictate to me, and I will search for some sort of artificial protection against it rather than face the risk of integrating that dark side with the rest of my personality. I may not feel that I count for much: but because to face that truth would be too destructive, I shelter behind those possessions, persons, even pets associated with me which have value and so indirectly confer value on me. ('Look at the way in which, despite me, my children have got on!') Churches have more than their share of those who are using the 'spiritual nature' of the institution in order to find shelter. The very strength of the institution can hinder the growth of that liberating self-awareness, which the freedom of the gospel is meant to inspire. The church then becomes a hindrance to growth and spirituality rather than its ally and its medium.

It is just such hindrances to self-awareness, such failures to implement human growth, that led to the formation of so many planned, intensive group experiences. Carl Rogers, their apostle, claims that they are 'the most rapidly spreading *social* invention of the century, and probably the most potent':[15] and, despite the way in which research into the results of such group-experiences has modified pretensions, many speak with evangelical fervour of the way in which such experiences have transformed their lives. I mean evangelical fervour: a fascinating parallel can be worked out between the way in which religious conversions and secular group experiences are described. Thomas Oden in his *Intensive Group Experience*[16] lists side by side startingly similar quotations from eighteenth and nineteenth century pietistic groups and current styles of group-encounter. I have a university extra-mural student in his late forties, an Anglican Reader, who claims that such group experience has enabled him for the first time in his life to start to love his fellow human beings.

Within such groups, expectations are that we shall come to let go the roles and pretensions we adopt in the world outside, and that genuine self-awareness, standing without our masks and props, and without the necessity to shelter behind some possession or institution, will emerge. If we are able to risk displaying our true feelings of weakness and inadequacy, our hatreds and dislikes, our fears and jealousies, we shall hope to meet with acceptance rather than the cold-shouldering we might expect in the society in which we move. That acceptance will help us not only to trust the group, but also to trust ourselves; and in trusting ourselves, our real selves, we shall come to see that we need not be afraid of self-awareness, since we have value as people quite apart from the defences and protections we gather round ourselves.

Few could deny the Christian 'tone' of such expectations, or even the language of honesty, trust, acceptance and love which the movement uses. Why, then, has there been a tendency in some church circles to ridicule the movement and use its more exotic manifestations (the high fees demanded, the sexual freedom encouraged) to laugh it out of court? Sometimes the reasons have been unworthy. Any attempt to undermine that polite conventional surface of pleasantness and 'niceness' which is the most dominant characteristic of some church life is seen as a threat personally and institutionally. The church's imperialistic claims to be able to know how to govern the whole of man's inner life, through the traditional apparatus of repentance and confession, often blind those within to the way in which such words remain just words. Perhaps the more perceptive will see these group-experiences as judgment, judgment on the way in which church life is meant to develop just those qualities claimed by the secular movement.

Slight experience of such groups provokes questions and hesitations about them – not all on account of the obstacles we erect and rationalize about in order to distance ourselves from self-knowledge. Christians will not find it easy, for instance, to go along with the over-optimistic view of human nature which lies behind them: to see the most evil manifestations of human nature, cruelty, sadism, torture as violent reactions against frustration of our intrinsic needs, and not as symptoms of a deep division within human nature, seems highly questionable. Again, whilst it may be true that Christians in particular are mesmerized by words and often use words to conceal rather than to express true feelings, the proper emphasis on the body to be found in such group-experiences should not blot out those searching questions which the mind needs to probe – even about the group-experience!

But perhaps the most fundamental difficulty presented to Christians is the presumption that I must ruthlessly pursue my

own growth – or indeed, *can* pursue my own growth – no matter
how other people may be hurt in the aggressive process the
group-experience sometimes implies. It is argued by those who
commend the group-experience that if we respect the defences
of another person, we are in the end deceiving him because we
are helping to perpetuate in him a system of illusions which can
only distance the person still further from his true self. There
may, certainly will, come a time when the defences of a particular person need to be penetrated by another person whom
they trust, if growth is to take place. There are equally occasions
when it would be morally wrong and positively harmful for
those defences to be pierced, especially by those whose knowledge of the other person has been very short.

All this should surely turn our attention to look again at the
opportunities which the fellowship of the church and established
church groups present to us. In chapter 4 of his letter to the
Ephesians, Paul speaks of our glorious destiny within the body
of Christ: that 'mature manhood, measured by nothing less than
the full stature of Christ'. And two verses further on, he
indicates how this might happen. 'Let us speak the truth in
love, so shall we fully grow up into Christ.' Of how many
churches could it be said that speaking the truth in love is one
of their distinguishing marks? It is easy, and gains some
insecure people notoriety, to be the sort of person who 'isn't
afraid to speak his mind': but 'speaking the truth in love'
equally implies 'listening to the truth in love' when others
speak it. I used to complain to my Parochial Church Council
when, after a meeting, I passed small groups of them huddled
under a street-light making points which they had not dared to
make inside: that is to deny the glorious opportunity for
example which the church possesses. There is the compelling
vision. A true *koinonia* of mature people who both speak and
listen to the truth in love. Disagreements can be expressed,
conflicts brought into the open – and the links of fellowship are
not broken. There is the strength of maturity. 'Fellowship' has
become synonymous with docility, pleasantness, a resistance to
change greater than we find elsewhere, a refusal to rock the boat,
a clinging to the shallow waters of convention and mediocrity.
Things might be so different. A group struggling to express the
maturity which is their goal both as Christians and as human

beings can be an example to many other human groups. Must it always be that secular movements catch us bathing and run away with our clothes?

Again, small group activities are increasingly becoming the most normal vehicle for the carrying on of the life of the church. Yet it is surely strange even within such small groups (let alone large church assemblies) how little opportunity there is for people to share with each other those pressing human needs they feel. The task so often becomes the business of *our* arranging something external to ourselves for *them* (the church overseas, the handicapped, and so on). The suggestion that we should look at relationships within the group, for instance, or consider the particular needs of one person within the group, would seem revolutionary to some. Yet the success of the intensive group movement is one indication of the failure of the church to provide the conditions for just that sort of sharing, and the failure is made more acute when Christians 'go overboard' for intensive-group experiences elsewhere and despair of the continuing church groups of which they are part.

The opportunities lie wherever the church exists as a small group, or in small groups, and no matter what its ostensible task may be. Secular group experiences differ because they are artificially constructed situations, in which strangers experience a great intensity of sharing in the short space of time – and then disperse. (No account seems to be taken of friendship in intensive group theory and practice.) A church grouping has within it the possibility of nurturing greater self-awareness in a setting which is longer-term and arises more naturally: a secular group is a fortuitous gathering of individuals with no reference beyond itself and the high expectations of those who compose it. Sharing, openness, trust, intimacy and worthwhileness probably best emerge as by-products of working together to achieve some common aim, where right attitudes are being developed. Hence, the pastor's task (learning from, but not swallowing neat, the intensive-group experience) will be to lead the group gently but firmly in the direction of greater self-disclosure, more honesty, a richer transparency. He will do it most frequently by his own self-disclosure, many disclaimers to infallibility, several attempts to display what is meant by being truly human. Quite apart from any advantage which may be his because of the 'naturalness' of the church group, he will not be working in a vacuum. He will be animated by the vision of the Kingdom of God towards which the group will be making its possibly minute contribution and the vision of God-in-Christ which he will see as the end for every member of the group. That, surprisingly, at first sight, will encourage him to be willing to allow the group to find its own answers; he will be an active participant not an authoritarian director; he will not be in despair when the group moves in a direction he would not have chosen; his trust in the group will be contagious. And he will have the inspiration of Jesus's method before him. He collected together one or two unpromising men, inspired them with a vision of God and of their possibilities, and built them into an intense fellowship with deep group-experience and a task to do.

Possibly the church concentrates too exclusively on the community, the fellowship, the togetherness of Christians. From the time of Jesus in the wilderness through St Antony in the Egyptian desert in the third century and on to Thomas Merton in his 'hermitage' in the twentieth century there have been those who have chosen and made aloneness the road to the vision of God. It was not that they thought of themselves as doing anything extraordinary: 'they had come into the desert to be themselves, their ordinary selves, and to forget a world that divided them from themselves'.[17] Paradoxically, as Thomas Merton found, withdrawal from the world brought him into closer relationship with it, because it nurtured the springs of his compassion.

There is abundant evidence that aloneness can provide rich soil in which the vision of God may flourish. There are many with whom the pastor is in touch who will have been made to feel (very often by other people) that to be alone is the ultimate disaster, that there is no difference between aloneness and loneliness. Some church people have been made to feel second-class Christians because they prefer the quietness of an early celebration of Holy Communion, where the emphasis is on the individual meeting with his Lord, rather than the more boisterous fellowship of the Parish Communion. But we were never meant to avoid the painful confrontation with ourselves which aloneness implies: here we can begin to look beyond both our own limitations and the boundaries of our existence. A pastoral task, then, is to be the agent of change from loneliness to solitude. Our first impulse is to arrange that people on their own should have company, and in some cases, that may be necessary. But we should never be guilty of implying that people are failures if they are alone, do not have a continuous round of parties, or adoring families. A most difficult, but rewarding piece of work is to help bring out resources in those who are alone to use their aloneness profitably: and perhaps in true monastic style, compassion and intercession for the world will be one of those resources. Difficult, rewarding – and enduring.

5

The Pastor as Educator

The word 'pastor' has not merely, as we have seen, a patronizing and paternalistic tone about it: it seems to spell protectiveness as well. This is felt to be especially true in the field of Christian adult education. Because educators introduce people to new and possibly subversive ideas, the pastor's role, it is assumed, is to see that the flock does not come to harm. The sheep must be kept in line, and protected from anything which might disturb their loyalty. The hysterical reaction of many in church first to *Honest to God*[1] and then fourteen years later to *The Myth of God Incarnate*[2] was very depressing because it illustrates a deep insecurity unworthy of a Christian attitude to truth. In any case, to believe that you can protect the simple faith of good folk from having their eyes opened to wider issues and possible doubts in the days of mass-communication, is not only undesirable but unrealistic as well. The old question, 'of what use is a faith that is never tested?' has educational implications as well as implications for living. Any examination of a church congregation reveals that those highly qualified in their jobs and often well-informed in other areas of life are at a very elementary stage in their understanding of Christian faith; and where they have progressed beyond the elementary stage, there is still a sense of unease, if not of downright dishonesty, because the present Christian environment often seems to prevent them from applying the same standards of enquiry, and handling the evidence in the same way as they do in their jobs. We have, however, so extolled the virtues of simple, unquestioning faith, so encouraged lay people in a passive, obedient role that we often fail to bring out into the open as we should the tensions people suffer between what they hear and say on Sundays and what they experience in the week. There is still abroad the notion that it is the job of the faithful to receive the truth which the authority of the church will dispense – and to receive it humbly.

Few are foolish enough to make that assumption too explicit, but it is significant that wherever lay people gather in conference, and whatever the formal agenda, one plea is made with great intensity: the plea for instruction, more definite teaching. There are frequent signs of some sort of aching lay-void, often inarticulately expressed, which, it is pathetically felt, 'proper teaching' or more authoritative statements from archbishops and the like will fill. In part, this may be nothing more than a thinly-disguised plea for handy dogmatic answers which will dispose of awkward questions; but it is also a sign of some deep disquiet that simple faith and lay people's experience of life are too far apart from each other. Indeed, the questions the alert layman faces are not necessarily those questions which traditional 'church teaching' will illuminate, or those subjects which have been regarded as essential for the trained clergyman.

We have already seen how little is needed by way of broad instruction in biblical knowledge: simply, the ability to use the Bible intelligently, see its different parts in perspective, and have right expectations of it. Or take another traditional key-subject, the history of Christian doctrine: could anyone argue that a detailed examination of early Christian heresies would necessarily be enlightening or nourishing for a strong Christian layman today? Or an exploration of the justification by faith controversy at the Reformation? Other questions may, and should, provoke him. In a country where there are now more Muslims than Methodists, how is he to relate what he has been taught to see as his unique faith with that of other religions? If no one comes to the Father but by Him, do we not have a duty to try and convert the others? These are sufficient grounds for unease, and hence for exploration: how legitimate, on Christian terms themselves, is mission in the twentieth century? And what of human relationships? The layman will hear much in church circles of insistence on 'Christian standards' and 'Christian principles' (even if such are not to be found in the New Testame.it!), as if those principles and standards were monolithic and self-evident. Rarely will he find a willingness to enter into the morally-grey area in which, were he to be honest, he would

admit he is constantly immersed. If relationships are to be ful-
filling, and relationship has been a key-word to some twentieth-
century theologians, then what relationships, and how far can
they be taken? What, too, of his Christian social responsibility?
The New Testament has little to say about the pressures great
institutions and technological enterprises exert on people, and
the perplexing questions they raise. Where is not only guidance
to be found, but also the opportunity given even to talk about
the problem?

If in this way the questions which come out of the layman's
daily experience provide the syllabus, rather than the simple
absorption of the 'received tradition', then the considerable
help which the adult Christian requires will not come to him
through the conventional teaching channels of the church.
Exposure to worship, however liturgically experimental, inevitably reinforces Christian 'imperialist' assumptions; the very
solemnity with which the Word is read continually raises false
expectations as to what Bible reading can accomplish; no public
pronouncement from the pulpit can deal adequately or sensi-
tively enough with the moral dilemmas posed in the real lives of
some of the congregation.

The logic seems inescapable. At the cost of sacrificing more
venerable activities (and the church often imagines that lay
people have unlimited time at their disposal) there needs to be
considerable expansion in the opportunities for adult education
in the church, comparable to those which have taken and are
taking place in the secular sphere. Richard Hoggart has recently
prophesied that 'continuing education' is likely to be the main
point of educational growth in the eighties. Will the church
catch up? 'If it ever was possible for a Christian to go through
the wilderness and storms of life like a camel, on the strength of
an education acquired as a child and haphazardly supplemented
by nibbling at sermons, that is a plain impossibility in a world
changing so rapidly. The churches have given to adult education
a very low status among their priorities, and the alienation of so
much adult thought from the world of the sermon has been the
penalty paid.'[3]

Concerned with personal growth, the pastor is bound to ask
how the local church programme needs to be re-orientated to
give proper pride of place to this adult education. It is not simply

or necessarily a matter of arranging groups to share common problems, 'parish weekends', 'teaching weeks', or even a multiplicity of house-groups, all of which have their place, but most of which have a middle-class flavour. It is certainly not a matter of arranging crash courses in 'Christian teaching' in the interests of 'lay-training'; if the word 'pastoral' is paternalistic, how much more so is 'lay-training'! The phrase bears so many wrong associations about Christian truth and communication, that perhaps it should be conveniently buried. It is a matter, primarily, of generating such a sense of freedom and openness that people of all sorts will try to express their convictions and reflect on what matters most to them in their faith, however inarticulately. (We often confuse conviction with the ability to be articulate.) That can be done in groups from varying social classes in ways that are different, and only perhaps suitable to that particular group. Eight or nine men from an east Manchester parish met regularly in their local once a month 'to chew things over', 'things' being difficulties they had experienced in being both industrial workers and church people. The conversation did not start with the Bible, but it was referred to before long.

Nor will the pastor look only to the church to provide what he is seeking. My own happy experience is that of working through a secular agency, a university extra-mural department, to provide education in religious studies for adult students from a wide variety of backgrounds and occupations. Now that might simply suggest a fact-imparting, examination-passing activity for those whose hobby is religion, especially since we are responsible for a two-year Certificate in Biblical Knowledge and a three-year Certificate in Religious Studies, as well as much course-provision in all aspects of those studies in different places of the region. Of course, there is a deal of suspicion in different quarters as to what we are really up to! Some less enlightened colleagues in other disciplines assume that we are in the business of fostering institutional aims and (however smoothly) disseminating religious propaganda: that increases our determination to show that like any other discipline, we are concerned with real educational needs and the rigorous pursuit of truth. Some more conservative-minded church colleagues suspect that we are seducing their good laymen by new-fangled ideas, and subverting the 'sound' teaching they are receiving from their pulpits on Sundays.

The facts are quite different. Far from being merely an information-imparting process, growth, in the sense in which we used the word in chapter 3, takes place, partly because of the nature of the provision which the secular agency provides. This can be illustrated from four different Christian perspectives on truth. First, in so far as truth is a matter of that which is intellectually understood, that which is grasped by the mind through concepts and arguments, the neutral setting in which such education takes place provides the opportunity for long-held assumptions really to be examined, possibly for the first time. Incidentally, it also provides the opportunity for Christians to meet and talk with and listen to those who do not share their convictions about Christian faith, a comparatively rare event. A surprising feature of secular provision is the number of those who are not Christians, but interested in questions of religious truth, who come to courses, and even wish to take certificates. I have a welcome 'thorn in the flesh' at the moment, a nursing-mother who is in the second year of her certificate course, and who, as an atheist, challenges all those assumptions which Christians make and are not properly thought out. A great deal of patience is needed to establish the atmosphere of confidence in which the Christian student can begin to expose his difficulties, and express the doubts which he might feel it strange, if not blasphemous, to mention, if he were in a church building. Very little experience is needed to see just how much conceptual lumber good church people find it necessary to carry around with them: the wealth of misunderstandings, the odd notions about what doctrinally is expected of Christians would be incredible if we did not know how little attention has been paid historically to Christian adult education. I remember well how at one meeting of a course on twentieth-century religious beliefs, a churchwarden was moved to say that although he had been coming to church for years, he had never discovered 'who God was' – and then, as if he had surprised himself by his willingness to be so courageous, he added, 'You know, that's the first time I've been able to say that.' At that point, although the course was half-over, real communication could begin. The ground had been cleared, and confidence established.

Truth is not only a matter of concept and logic, of discussion and clarification: it is secondly, something intuitively apprehended, an illumination or disclosure. This brings us back to Ian Ramsey's idea of religious education as providing the opportunity through which such disclosures might occur. It also takes us to Mary Warnock's view that 'a good education must, above all things, be directed towards the strengthening of the faculty of imagination.' 'Imagination is that which will enable us to perceive things, as Wordsworth did, for their own sake, and for the sake of what lies beyond them.'[4] This is where religious studies finds allies in other disciplines: the use of the medium of visual art and literature, for instance. A most fruitful, if incidental, experiment in adult education in my experience was that of a recent Arts Festival for the community, pioneered by a church near Oxford. Local people contributed all kinds of handiwork, pottery and painting, and it was a considerable exercise in encouraging latent talents and in appreciation of new creativity in each other: there was another way to 'open the eyes of the blind'. Perhaps it is just as much the business of Christian adult education to provide spaces for reflection, where horizons can be stretched, and illumination and disclosure might take place as it is to promote formal courses in 'Bible-knowledge'. The sad fact is that whilst, in my experience, these latter prosper numerically, church people are much more hesitant about the other sort, which they consider not 'really Christian'. Perhaps only a renewed emphasis on vision will help us alter course, and this would seem an urgent matter in view of the increasingly fundamentalist strain of much contemporary Christianity.

A third perspective on truth is what John calls 'doing the truth'. 'Truth in Christianity,' says Paul Tillich, 'is something which *happens*, something which is bound to a special place, to a special time, to a special personality . . . The mystery of truth in Christianity is an event which has taken place and which takes place again and again. It is life, personal life, revelation and decision.'[5] There is a working-out, in other words, in practical terms of that life which is always being drawn towards the vision of God, through informal workshops on moral and ethical themes. One of the most worthwhile ventures we have organized has been a series of such workshops in a labour club in an area of the city undergoing vast demolition. Another recent, if controversial, workshop has been that which has explored a Christian view of homosexuality. Given imagination and the willingness to take risks, the means of adult education are many and multifarious. It is not a matter of placing secular and church provision in opposition to each other; secular provision often suffers, too, from conservatism, bureaucratic muddle, inefficiency and lack of vision. It is simply the business of being ready to use the means which seem most appropriate, in a given situation, to nurture education, and hence personal growth.

Truth is also discovered, finally, for oneself and about oneself in the companionship of others in a shared experience. This perspective we have glanced at before when we looked at the phenomenon of groups. David Jenkins has recently pointed out how 'corporate community knowledge and experience has tended to be greatly neglected or discouraged in Western Christian tradition and especially in modern Protestantism'.[6] He pleads for a return to a form of knowing which comes not on a narrowly intellectualist route but from the current situations and common experience of believers. 'God is known to be God because he establishes himself as God in the experience, response and tradition of those who understand themselves, their hopes and the world in relation to him.'[7] The community of the church, simply as community, can be a powerful educational resource. The practical problem is the staleness often evident amongst smaller groups within the wider community of the church. If at some stage the level of group-experience has been high, the group does not want to split up, and suffers a feeling of impending bereavement. In my view, groups should always be temporary, and ready to disperse at the right moment: the mediocrity of church life is sometimes attributable to the continued existence of groups which should have been dissolved years ago.

The pastor, then, will be as pastor a concerned educator, or at least, one who points others to make best use of all the educational facilities available. As a facilitator of growth, he will see no divergence between his aim as pastor and his aim as educator. In both he is, however indirectly, a stimulator of vision. He will be very alive to the dangers of the educational short-cut which in the end ceases to be education and becomes indoctrination:

R. M. Hare was speaking in the following context of children's education, but it has a direct relevance, too, for adults:

> The educator is trying to turn children into adults: the indoctrinator is trying to make them into perpetual children. The educator is waiting and hoping all the time for those whom he is educating to start *thinking*; and none of the thoughts that may occur to them are labelled 'dangerous' a priori. The indoctrinator, on the other hand, is watching for signs of trouble, and ready to intervene to suppress it when it appears, however oblique and smooth his methods may be. The difference between these two is like the difference between the colonial administrator who knows, and is pleased, that he is working himself out of a job, and the one who is determined that the job shall still be there even when he himself retires.
>
> So there is, in the end, a very great difference between the two methods. At the end of it all, the educator will insensibly stop being an educator, and find that he is talking to an equal, to an educated man like himself – a man who may disagree with everything he has ever said; and, unlike the indoctrinator, he will be pleased. So, when this happens, you can tell from the expression on his face which he is.[8]

I have been suggesting that through adult education, Christians can win through to seeing that the proper failure of the church to provide the easy answers which its dogmatic position presupposes is not failure at all, but the secret of Christian living. They can begin to learn to live alongside agnostics and atheists with a greater degree of honesty and understanding. It may be, as Harvey Cox has argued, that behind all our failures in religion today, 'there is the numbing and anaesthetising of the psyche which is the price our civilization has paid for industrial affluence and the technical mastery of the world.'[9] In so far, however, as Christian faith is rejected and ignored because it does not seem to connect in any real way with the experience which many people have of life today, adult education has a major role to play. Here education and evangelism meet – with integrity.

There is another particularly apt educational task for the minister as pastor today: that of encouraging lay people to share some of his own insights into effective pastoral care, and so of properly channelling their keennness to love other people as themselves. There are plenty of untapped resources of goodwill within our churches, and many people are looking for ways in which to be more realistically helpful to one another. In trying to bring together the considerable resources for helping within the community to bear on the equally considerable human problems which beset society, we cannot simply depend on the caring professions. There needs to be encouragement given to other people to use their own resources as human beings, since most human needs can be and have been met by those who are not professionals. The purpose is not to train amateur psychologists, psychiatrists or sociologists. It is to give opportunity to reflect at some depth on what being a helper is, to provide some background and support. A new terminal-care hospice in Manchester has had no difficulty in calling out a lengthy list of volunteers. They are looked upon primarily as practical helpers, but because they will be talking with patients, and in some small way entering into patients' situations, they will need some guidance – even if it is only in a negative sense, of what not to say! The wider purpose is to lead to greater understanding of basic human needs, of how we relate to one another, how we can sustain one another in areas of depression, marital conflict, dying and bereavement. This is almost certain to lead to greater sensitivity to Christian faith, since that faith will be seen in the context of real and pressing needs.

This important task, of the sharing of pastoral wisdom, can be done at many different levels. For myself, two of the most recent worthwhile ventures in which I have taken part have been amongst a group of Free Church ministerial students and lay leaders from local churches learning together about the 'helping process' and an extra-mural course, again with students with a wide variety of experience, on 'being good neighbours'. As a result of this course, one adult student has decided to write a thesis (involving reading and reflections on her own experience) about the pastoral care of the elderly. So interest, care and expertise grow as the pastor draws out appropriate human skills and nourishes richer community life within the church, which in its turn can be used as a powerful resource within the wider community itself.

6

The Pastor as Counsellor and Helper

If the pastor is a professional, in what does his professionalism consist? Envious of the professional status afforded to the medical and some of the other caring professions, and uncertain of our role, our inclination is often to ape what we feel to be the essence of their professionalism. Traditionally, that has been based on the existence of a so-called knowledge or competence-gap between doctor and patient. 'We are the experts: we know what is best for you: you put yourself entirely in our hands, and meekly submit to what we ask of you.' The attitude is well illustrated in the recent play by Brian Clark, *Whose Life is it Anyway?* in which the chief character, Ken, a sculptor, has been the victim of a severe road accident, and is paralysed from the neck down. The hospital doctors take it for granted that once his condition is stabilized, he will be transferred to another unit, and so techincally-speaking, be kept alive. Ken, with ice-cool clarity, argues from his bed that he should be allowed to die. Dr Emerson, the consultant physician, is about to inject Ken with valium.

> Ken: Hello, hello, they've brought up the heavy brigade.
> (Dr Emerson pulls back the bed clothes and reaches for Ken's arm.)
> Dr Emerson, I am afraid I must insist that you do not stick that needle in me.
> Dr Emerson: It is important that I do.
> Ken: Who for?
> Dr Emerson: You.
> Ken: I'm the best judge of that.
> Dr Emerson: I think not. You don't even know what's in this syringe.

Ken: I take it that the injection is one of a series of
measures to keep me alive.
Dr Emerson: You could say that.
Ken: Then it is not important. I've decided not to
stay alive.
Dr Emerson: But you can't decide that.
Ken: Why not?
Dr Emerson: You're very depressed.[1]

The character Kostoglotov in Solzhenitsyn's novel *Cancer Ward*
similarly complains to Dontsova, the doctor:

You see, you start from a completely false position. No sooner
does a patient come to you than you begin to do all his
thinking for him. After that, the thinking's done by your
standing orders, your five-minute conferences, your programme, your plan and the honour of your medical department. And once again I become a grain of sand, just like I
was in the camp. Once again nothing *depends* on me.[2]

Sidney Jourard in his book, *The Transparent Self* criticizes this
model which is dependent on a competence-gap not simply
because it does not allow the healer to be 'authentic', but because
it actively works against that healing process he is otherwise
aiming to promote through physical means. The response to
sickness becomes a stereotyped mode of behaviour known as the
'bedside manner', a benevolent and cheerful despotism. This
bedside manner serves the professional's interest more than the
patient's. It is a defence against feeling threatened and helpless.
But it is also bound to exclude a source of information as vital to
the patient's recovery as his temperature, blood pressure or any
other physical indication: that is, what is on his mind. Physical
instruments reveal the state of the patient's body: being able to
talk reveals something of the state of the patient as a whole. If
the patient has something on his mind, almost certainly it will
be a factor in his general health But the bedside manner will
not encourage its release; it suppresses individuality, and
attempts to bring about a uniformity of reaction in patients, so
that the professional can feel 'safe'. 'I know of several instances
of people who nearly died because every time they tried to tell
their nurse of their intolerance of penicillin, the nurse replied,

cheerfully and firmly, as she neatly performed the injection, "The doctor knows what's best; this will help to get you well." Nobody listened.'[3] When in critical situations, the patient has a chance of being listened to, by members of the other caring professions, very often his attention is diverted anywhere so long as it is away from the real situations he passionately wishes to explore. Especially in terminal illness, patients find it extraordinarily difficult to find those who are prepared to let them express all their fears and anxieties, to penetrate the 'deathly' silence with which they are surrounded. There is a poignant and humorous illustration of this in *Whose Life is it Anyway?* Mrs Gillian Boyle is 'thirty-five, attractive, and very professional in her manner. She is a medical worker.'

   Mrs Boyle: Good morning.
      Ken: Morning.
   Mrs Boyle: Mr Harrison?
      Ken: (cheerfully) It used to be.
   Mrs Boyle: My name is Mrs Boyle.
      Ken: And you've come to cheer me up.
   Mrs Boyle: I wouldn't put it like that.
      Ken: How would you put it?
   Mrs Boyle: I've come to see if I can help.
      Ken: Good. You can.
   Mrs Boyle: How?
      Ken: Go and convince Dr Frankenstein that he has successfully made his monster and he can now let it go.
   Mrs Boyle: Dr Emerson is a first-rate physician. My goodness, they have improved this room.
      Ken: Have they?
   Mrs Boyle: It used to be really dismal. All dark green and cream. It's surprising what pastel colours will do, isn't it? Really cheerful.
      Ken: Yes; perhaps they should try painting me. I'd hate to be the thing that ruins the decor.[4]

As the conversation proceeds, and Ken's frustrations make him more bitter:

      Ken: It's marvellous you know.
   Mrs Boyle: What is?

Ken: All you people have the same technique. When I say something really awkward you just pretend I haven't said anything at all. You're all the bloody same . . . Well there's another outburst. That should be your cue to comment on the light-shade or the colour of the walls.

Mrs Boyle: I'm sorry if I have upset you.

Ken: Of course you have upset me. You and the doctors with your appalling so-called profes-sionalism, which is nothing more than a series of verbal tricks to prevent you relating to your patients as human beings.

Mrs Boyle: You must understand; we have to remain rela-tively detached in order to help . . .

Ken: That's alright with me. Detach yourself. Tear yourself off on the dotted line that divides the woman from the social worker and post yourself off to another patient.

Mrs Boyle: You're very upset . . .

Ken: Christ Almighty, you're doing it again. Listen to yourself woman. I say something offensive about you and you turn your professional cheek. If you were human, if you were treating me as human, you'd tell me to bugger off. Can't you see that this is why I've decided that life isn't worth living? I am not human and I'm even more convinced of that by your visit than I was before, so how does that grab you? The very exercise of your so-called professionalism makes me want to die.[5]

Later on in the day, Ken has a word to say about the chaplain.

He was in here the other day. He seemed to think that I should be quite happy to be God's chosen vessel into which people could pour their compassion . . . That it was alright being a cripple because it made other folk feel good when they helped me.[6]

In a vain attempt to establish professional status along with the desire for self-protection, pastors, too, distance themselves from people in pastoral relationships, or attempt to cover over chasms of suffering, pain and anxiety with enforced cheerfulness. There are different masks we can put on and take off when we meet people whose problems seem intractable. We can hide behind religious phrases like, 'God's chosen vessel'; behind dog-collars, which give us at least an air of professionalism; behind the sacraments and prayers which it is also our professional privilege to administer. A religious stance, and religious functions can be used as defences against costly personal involvement, against real encounters with people in stark situations. There is an ambiguity in religion which the pastor always needs to recognize: it can open him up or shield him from God's reality.

In any case, an unreal (and often, harmful) distinction is often made between 'helper' and 'helped'. The adoption of the helping role (doing something *to* or *for* somebody) can lead not only to patronizing, but also to arrogance, quite apart from the way in which it can blind us to the reason many of us chose to be helpers in the first place: in order to be helped! Once we take this to heart, we shall not make the mistake of feeling that it is the 'strong' who help the 'weak'. It is those who are willing to let go pretences who help most. Monica Furlong's poem, 'A slum is where somebody else lives' makes this point:

> A slum is where somebody else lives,
> Help is what others need.
> We all want to be the priest, social worker, nurse,
> The nun in the white habit giving out the soup –
> To work from a position of power,
> The power being
> That we are not the shuffler in the queue
> Holding out his bowl.
> But there is only one way into the kingdom
> – To be found out in our poverty.
> That is why the citizens are a job lot –
> Unhappily married, the feckless mother of eight,
> The harlot no longer young,
> The lover of little girls, the sexually untameable,
> The alcoholic, the violent, and those whose drink is despair.
> Show me not, Lord, your rich men

With their proud boasts of poverty and celibacy
They are too much for me.
Hide me from those who want to help
And still have strength to do so.
Only those who get on with their lives
And think they have nothing to give
Are any use to me.
Let your bankrupts feed me.[7]

The paradox seems to be not only that there is no helping without being helped, but also that sometimes it is when we are feeling most unhelpful, even helpless, that we are of most help – providing we do not shrink from the feeling of helplessness, and attempt to minimize it by an attitude of defensiveness. The mode of Jesus's ministry, chosen in the wilderness, contained within it this potential of helplessness. In Gethsemane, that choice is reaffirmed, and then he experiences the physical helplessness of torture and crucifixion and the mental and spiritual helplessness of feeling abandoned by his father, expressed in his cry of dereliction. He dies, powerless, helpless – by choice. His death is a direct result of the decision he had taken in the wilderness, and pursued throughout his ministry. Yet it was at the point of helplessness that God seemed to bring new meaning out of his life. The victory of the resurrection is in part, a victory of the way of helplessness, a confirmation of the mode of Jesus's ministry. The glory of God is seen, not in contrast to helplessness, but through it.

It is, then, an inadequate view of the pastor to see him always as the strong, helping hand. In any case, it is a common experience to be both strong and weak, in different areas and at different times; to be devastatingly shaky in some situations, and almost rock-like in others. Glib assumptions about caring constantly need to be challenged: the four-letter word 'help' is deceptively simple. Pastoral ministry is a sharing of self-understanding, and an invitation to the other person to risk that sharing. Helplessness and suffering are part of the human condition, to be avoided if possible, but never at the cost of authenticity or integrity. To be ready to acknowledge and live with helplessness, it is essential for the pastor to keep clear his vision of God-in-Christ, and live close to the source of his ministry.

He may not feel very expert in the ways of prayer as tradi-tionally described. Here, too, he may feel weak, if not helpless. Again, neither success nor expertise is of much account. What matters is the attempt he makes, in his own way, to keep open and warm his relationship with God, no matter how fragile it appears on occasions and no matter how much anger he may wish on occasions to express in his prayers! Other people often sense very quickly when alleged Christian professionals have given up trying to live close to the source of their ministry. The pastor who stills prays (or tries to) is far more significant than the 'dynamic', the 'socially-involved' or the liturgical whizz-kid. Perhaps, too, his willingness to talk about his own difficulties in praying may often help those who have similar difficulties to talk more freely and honestly with him. Honesty is fundamental, not just about prayer, but about Christian faith as a whole. Relations within churches would be much more productive and healthy if pastors were prepared to say where they doubted, to admit that in certain circumstances there is no easy Christian answer, even if there is one at all. But this is only to repeat that the heart of the matter is journeying towards the goal of vision rather than a 'credal package', or even a 'morality package' which we have inherited. 'Christian life is an adventure, a voyage of discovery, a journey, sustained by faith and hope, towards a final and complete communion with the Love at the heart of all things.'[8]

It is this vision which the pastor will be indirectly com-municating through the attitude he adopts in his pastoral relationships, even though there may be no legitimate oppor-tunity for explicit references to Christ. All counselling theory and experience would suggest that it is the personality of the therapist himself which is the chief catalyst in the process of healing and growth. So it is not so much a matter of learning pastoral techniques, as of nurturing human qualities. This is not to say that a certain technical competence is not necessary in a pastor, just as one would ask for competence in a butcher! Asking for help is scaring, and a certain efficiency is helpful, especially in the first approaches. It is just that competence and efficiency by themselves, do not make the pastor.

Carl Rogers specifies three qualities essential to the pastoral counsellor. They are empathy, caring and genuineness.

Empathy is the business of trying to get inside the world of another person, feeling what it is like to be him or her at that moment, 'as if' you were him or her (without transgressing the boundary the words 'as if' draw). This implies the giving the whole of one's attention to another person, in particular through the ministry of listening, the hardest of arts and yet the most therapeutic. Bonhoeffer saw this clearly:

> It is his work we do for our brother when we learn to listen to him. Christians, especially ministers, so often think they must always contribute something when they are in the company of others, that this is the one service they have to render. They forget that listening can be a greater service than speaking. Many people are looking for an ear that will listen. They do not find it among Christians, because these Christians are talking where they should be listening . . . In the end there is nothing left but spiritual chatter and clerical condescension arrayed in pious words.[9]

I wonder how far our stress on the words of Jesus has led to a distorted view of the way in which he must have shown himself to individuals as the most sensitive of listeners and hence the most empathetic of characters?

The second quality is caring: Rogers says that he prefers the word 'prizing', the way a parent prizes a child. This is not necessarily to show approval of everything the child says and does, but to affirm the child's *worth*. Similarly, the counsellor affirms the worth of the other person, indicates that he has value even though at that time he may be so totally confused and his life such a jumble of contradictions that he feels he cannot be of use to anyone. Perhaps the giving of an hour's time simply to listen is to say effectively a great deal about the worth of another person. It may be the first occasion in their lives when they have been given the chance to know that what they feel and do and are *matters*, given the space to reflect in the company of another on their own *value*. Jesus said, 'Are not sparrows two a penny? Yet without your Father's leave not one of them falls to the ground. As for you, the hairs of your head have all been counted. So have no fear: you are worth more than any number of sparrows' (Matt. 10.29–31).

The third quality is genuineness, being without facade, and

without any spurious white-coated professionalism. Genuineness, a real expression of what it is I am experiencing when I am in a pastoral relationship with another, is to take a risk and make myself vulnerable. It becomes easier as professional life goes on, to suppress more and more of the real self, to behave as we are expected to behave and feel what we should feel. But it is those 'real selves' which offer the richest resources, so we shall not be afraid of showing, for instance, simple human *warmth*, which seems to arouse such suspicion in those who work in the caring professions. It need not detract from a proper sense of detachment and can, when genuinely felt and expressed, release tension in a way nothing else can. It is the genuine giving of a genuine self which is the most we have to offer. Does not that take us right to the heart of Jesus? Again, the phrase which forms part of the 'received gospel' of social workers – acceptance of the client – can be seen as having its roots in the quality of acceptance displayed by Jesus, and in the freedom he always seems to have given to his friends to make their own decisions about their lives.

Christian criticism of this counselling stance often rests on the way it does not seem to allow for that judgment or denunciation of sin which, it is argued, occupies a central place in the dealings Jesus had with individuals. The contention is superficial. There is in the unconditional love implicit in this stance a judgment far more real and searching than any words of judgment which even if the pastor felt it right to utter (and that is doubtful) would distance the other person from him. Time and time again, we wish to modify that full belief in the power of unconditonal love the gospel implies: we often wish to reserve to our use some small bit of power of uttering the 'authoritative word' because we are not as fully convinced as we ought to be of the power of persuasive love, the strongest force in the world. The sad experience of many counsellors is that most people are only too willing to judge themselves – and not just those with a religious faith. It is naive to think that people have no sense of self-judgment until a 'word of judgment' is spoken. The real difficulty is how in the short term to help those who have a strong sense of guilt and are severe in their own self-condemnation but whose lack of faith prevents the effective use of any narrowly 'religious' resource, like confession and absolution. (Albert

Camus' novel *The Fall* illustrates this problem.) Perhaps the most the pastor can do here is to help a more balanced assessment of the situation, and prevent the person concerned from falling overboard into a sea of self-hatred.

The first implication of all this for the pastor is obvious to see, yet subtle in its ability to creep into our dealings stealthily and unawares. We shall be concerned with the maturity of those with whom we are in touch, not their dependence. We will always want to ensure their freedom to disagree with us, to go for help elsewhere, to make their own decisions, even to reject us. This may make for an uncomfortable life, but the insidious danger of dependence is far deadlier (and of course, we all seek some measure of dependence, someone on whom to trust and lean). If we pursue the doctor-patient model, we may undermine the ability of people to deal with their own human condition and weakness in a personal and autonomous way. We may reduce them to the status of passive and dependent consumers who are no longer taking any part in their own treatment and healing.

Not only must we refuse to take over the running of someone else's life, but we must continually ask ourselves why it is that we are attracted by allowing others to be dependent on us. Is it the power we have, or are we using the other person and the help and care we offer as a very effective way of hiding from ourselves our own considerable deep personal needs?

The second implication is connected with the first: namely, that we shall in our pastoral relationships always treat people as if they were mature. This is a difficult truth to substantiate and demonstrate, and I can only claim that it comes out of my own rather painful experience There are many temptations to short-circuit problems, by imposing solutions of our own, because we think we know best. Confronted by what is obviously feckless ignorance or unintelligence, we can easily persuade ourselves that it would be folly to let the decision-making go out of our hands. If as pastors we are also concerned with the welfare of the church as an institution, there is also considerable pressure on us subtly to manipulate and dictate to people for the church's sake. But in the end, this is just another facet of our inner urge to keep people dependent. As parents painfully come to see, growth happens when children are allowed to make mistakes, and are still supported through those mistakes. The bigger the heart of the pastor, the more he will wish for the magic wand which will dissolve the difficulties and sufferings of those whom he is with at a stroke – and the more important, if not indispensable, he will in consequence, feel. (I will always be grateful to the first organist with whom I served, who once took me out to the graveyard surrounding the church, and said rather gloomily, 'That place is full of indispensables!') It is difficult to live with *apparent* impotence – but it is only apparent. The most the pastor may be able to do with someone eaten up by loneliness is to help the person accept their lonelines as part of what it means to be a human being. He cannot, like a doctor, prescribe tranquillizers for the pain. Again, there is no point, and possibly evasion, in simply listing compensations a bereaved person may have (other relatives, children, a secure place in the neighbourhood, and so on) when the basic problem is that of coming to terms with the loss which death has brought. There may be some little place for 'temporizing', but if it continues indefinitely, it is treating adults as children, and keeping them immature.

I have argued that any adequate model of pastoral help must depend on the vulnerability, self-disclosure (and sometimes helplessness) of the pastor himself, that his qualities of genuine empathetic care are his best resources. We can test this, for instance, in a difficult situation with which we as pastors have to deal: the pastoral care of those who have been suddenly bereaved, through a coronary thrombosis or road accident. Dying and bereavement have become important topics for psychologists, sociologists and others working in medicine. At one level, at least, the conspiracy of silence seems to have been broken. Research carried out over the past fifteen years, associated with the names of Elizabeth Kübler-Ross and Colin Murray Parkes, has established some general pattern of bereavement, with certain well-defined stages. The first stage, obviously, is that of numbness and denial. The bereaved person cannot take in the fact of the death, and this seems to have little to do with whether the person has died suddenly or slowly. The period can last as long as a month, but is usually about a week. In this state of shock, when the numbness is heightened often by the generous use of tranquillizers, even though practical arrangements have to be made about the funeral and the immediate future, rational conversation may scarcely be possible. What is the resource that the pastor can offer? Obviously, it will not be words (which will not communicate, in any case) or any short-cuts to healing. Bonhoeffer's distinction between the ultimate and penultimate word is most relevant in this situation:

> When I am with someone who has suffered a bereavement, I often decide to adopt a 'penultimate' attitude, particularly when I am dealing with Christians, remaining silent as a sign that I share in the bereaved man's helplessness in the face of such a grievous event, and not speaking the biblical words of comfort which are, in fact, known to me and available to me. Why am I often unable to open my mouth, when I ought to give expression to the ultimate? And why, instead, do I decide on an expression of thoroughly penultimate human solidarity? Is it from mistrust of the power of the ultimate word? Is it from fear of men? Or is there some good positive reason for such an attitude, namely, that my knowledge of the word, my having it at my finger-tips, in other words my being, so to speak, spiritually master of the situation, bears only the appearance of the ultimate, but is in reality itself something entirely penultimate? Does one not in some cases, by remaining deliberately in the penultimate, perhaps point all the more genuinely to the ultimate, which God will speak in His own time (though indeed even then through a human mouth)?[10]

Our only resource will be our exposed selves. The bereaved will take from our presence, from the depths of what they have known of us or see in us, something of what they need at that particular time. It is not so much formal religion even the committed are looking for then. It is the assurance that still, in the midst of their loss, all is well, and this is communicated by presence, by our sense of inner peace but not complacency, by our looks, by our touch. Someone recently said to me that the person who helped her most when she had found her father dead and failed with the 'kiss of life' was someone who just held her hand for a whole afternoon whilst she shook with what would hardly come out as tears. Presence releases as well as comforts, and it will communicate our willingness to receive whatever the bereaved feels like expressing at that moment. (Incidentally, how much we are conditioned to bottle things up and keep things under, for the sake of other people. It is an odd irony that the one who is suffering most often thinks more of the 'helpers' and so restrain the tears.)

Perhaps *absorb* is the one word which catches best the attitude I seek to describe: to be able to absorb other people's feelings without reflecting them is a great pastoral gift. In Susan Hill's moving novel of a young widow, Ruth, and her first year of sudden bereavement, *In the Springtime of the Year*,[11] it is her younger brother-in-law, Jo, who does quietly the practical jobs that need to be done – making the tea, lighting the fire, collecting the eggs – but who says least and absorbs most Ruth's moods of anger, guilt and frustration. Pastors need to be able to absorb other people's depressions, and today, especially, they may have to absorb a lot from people who feel they have been hurt or abandoned by the church. Absorption is at the heart of so much pastoral method, and certainly of forgiveness. Jesus on the cross absorbed all the feelings of hatred which were loosed upon him, and his response, 'Father, forgive them, for they do not know what they are doing', stopped the power of evil to produce more evil.

Continuing to absorb someone's pain and anger is infinitely tiring, and the costliness of the situation, our lack of confidence that God works through our abiding in Christ, will make us want to cut the business short, using old clichés, dragging in religious concepts to relieve us rather than help the bereaved. Above all, pastoral ministry to the suddenly bereaved implies that we ourselves have recognized the blessedness of life's limitations and the boundary which death provides, and which makes every day worth while. It implies that we have come to terms as fully as possible with our own dying and death. That is our support when we are alongside the bereaved, with them, in their weakness – and in ours.

7

The Pastor and the Kingdom

How right are we to spend so much time involved in the details of one person's life? Is it not a luxury in a world where for every hour we spend like this another half-dozen children somewhere will die through starvation? Indeed, perhaps some of those personal problems would shrink and begin to disappear if attention were diverted outwards towards helping cure basic human problems of need, rather than turned inwards on sophisticated personal dilemmas.

The issues are not so clear-cut. Attending to individuals and their needs is never a luxury, and is basic to all improvement of the human lot. It is interesting, for instance, that Gandhi, whom we remember primarily as a social reformer in a country beset by some of the gravest problems historical experience and the environment could produce, believed passionately that you could in the long run only change institutions, structures, economic conditions and relations by what he called a 'change of heart' among individuals. In the Indian situation, he might well have been expected to concentrate exclusively on structures, and this is what the other politicians wanted him to do. But he spent an enormous amount of time on what quite properly could be called 'pastoral care' through letters, his ashram, books and newspapers. He covered a wide range of subjects concerning the lives of ordinary people but which most politicians did not consider to be concerned with politics at all. He saw a vital connection, for instance, between religion and sanitation.[1] Again, there is enough tragic evidence around today of what happens amongst devoted missionaries who are exhausting themselves trying to cope with Third World problems and structures and have not begun to face themselves and their own inability to relate to one another.

Nevertheless, the temptation of the pastorally-inclined (I see it in myself) is always to exaggerate the extent to which individuals can be helped regardless of the circumstances in which political, social and economic realities place them. We need to remember that structures have a value, for without them, not even basic relationships can be established. Sweeping away structures will only, in the end, lead to more structures. The liberation of persons which is the aim of pastoral care cannot of itself solve the complex issues of the world any more than the preaching and acceptances of the evangelical message of the gospel will necessarily cure our social ills. All the human sciences increasingly throughout the twentieth century have pointed us to the subtle interplay between man and his environment: that I am not merely involved with mankind, but reflect, and am partially determined by the network of all the personal and social circumstances in which I find myself. It is within this setting, not amongst a series of isolated individuals, that the pastor's work is to operate. Set against the desperate situations in which some people find themselves, through no fault of their own, a concern for my salvation, or even my self-actualization, represents a staggering selfishness from which in turn I may need to be liberated.

That selfish concern for 'salvation', the notion that we sit down and brood with furrowed brows over the state of our own souls, is a travesty of Christian faith – a travesty that could only happen when what Pannenberg calls ' "the resounding motif" of Jesus' message', the imminent Kingdom of God, has become obscured. If the pursuit of the vision of God is the key to the Christian's motivation and perseverence, the call of the Kingdom provides his dynamic and is complementary to that vision. Perhaps we have insufficiently seen that Christian motivation is as much to do with a longing for the realization of what is to be in the future, as with gratitude for what it has received of God's mercy and forgiveness in the past. The phrase 'the Kingdom of God' occurs more than eighty times in the first three gospels, and the flexibility with which Jesus uses it (which explains its compelling attraction) has led several to imprison its meaning in that which can be pin-pointed: for instance, in the visible church or in a reformed social order. It relates to both these, has implications for them, but is bigger and wider than both of them. If it were not, it could not be the resource and inspiration it potentially represents. It is a powerful incentive in history, but is never achieved in history. Some contemporary scholars tell us that C. H. Dodd's classic work, *The Parables of the Kingdom*[2] which stressed 'realised eschatology' minimized the idea of 'futurity' of the Kingdom in the New Testament as a remnant of Jewish thought. Yet such 'futurity is fundamental for Jesus' message'.[3]

> The utter realism of the Biblical literature is evident in its proclamation of the Kingdom of God as the *coming* reality. No matter how well things were going, no matter how intimately the communion with God was felt, the Kingdom of God was announced as the future, the coming, Kingdom.[4]

Parallel to the pursuit of the vision of God, it is an invitation to become fellow-workers in a task in which every detail is always worthwhile, but which is never to be consummated. When we have done all, we still have to say we are unprofitable servants. But the Kingdom is still worthy of our sacrificial efforts.

Utopias have usually had a bad press in Christian circles, largely on the grounds that they do not take account of man's sin and corruption. But they have persisted in history – from Plato through Thomas More to Karl Marx – and perhaps before being too derisory, we need to ask why they have persisted. William Blake's 'Jerusalem' and even J. Addington Symond's

> These things shall be! A loftier race
> Than e'er the world hath known, shall rise
> With flame of freedom in their souls
> And light of science in their eyes.

(contemptuously dismissed as Victorian optimism or as facile belief in evolutionary progress) strike a powerful chord in many people despite the 'correctness' of the theological strictures imposed on them. A brief excursion into Marxism confirms this view. Commentators have often alluded to the messianic strain in Karl Marx's thought, thanks to his Jewish ancestry. Certainly, he never abandoned his vision of a Utopia, even if in his later years it faded a little: a society where because the means of production were in the right hands, man's alienation from his fellow-men would be at an end, and man's creativity in the realm of science and art and human relationships would flourish. Who could measure the effect that the vision of a classless society has had in our century?

Marx saw bourgeois society with all its contradictions as a society *in the process of becoming*. He dreamed of communism as a society that had completed this process. He did not expect communism to be the simple negation of private property but its positive abolition in a world of plenty, of humanity and integrated intelligence: 'the real appropriation of human nature through and for man'.[5]

At the age of twenty-one, Marx had criticized the self-centredness of many philosophies: 'Thus, when the universal sun has set, doth the moth seek the lamp-light of privacy.'[6] We need, Marx thought, to be called out of ourselves by that which goes beyond our narrow private concerns: not to 'revolve forever inside our own skins' but to contribute to the transformation of society. The appeal of Marxism can never be understood if its commitment to a vision of a just order of society, its Utopian 'dream of the whole man', is not taken seriously. That 'dream' and the practical consequences that have flowed from it should alert radical Christians to the dangers of a simple immersion in 'political realism', which over-simplifies the issues, and fails to gain that sense both of perspective and direction which right political action demand.

Sadly, but significantly, there is little contemporary contribution being made to political theory in a world of political pragmatism. Possibly that lack of political theory is part of a wider problem of contemporary Western European philosophy: namely, the impossibility of 'seeing a thing whole' (whatever the problem under review) because we are so concerned with the problem of knowledge, how one knows it at all, and what it is possible to know. The whole notion of vision seems at odds with the current climate of philosophical endeavour. We need perhaps to learn from the East and in particular from a man like Gandhi, who was free to 'see', just because he was not influenced by the philosophical constrictions of others in the West. Our most pressing need is the lifting of the political debate in this country to a point from which at least some of the heights can be seen and aspired to. That traditionally has been the task of political theorists: and it is no accident that Christians and Christian faith have made an important contribution. (Where are they today?) There must always be a way of 'seeing' in politics – not just in the sense of 'seeing' what actually is, but also in the sense of judging what is against a vision. Just as the teaching of Jesus was coloured by hyperbole to stretch horizons and stab people awake, so political theorists have often used exaggeration and extravagances in order to open man's eyes to see that which otherwise they would miss. Such a vision is important because political theory, rightly understood, can begin to lessen the gap between the possibilities imagination can discern and the practicalities of day-to-day political life.

It is just such a commitment, to the transformation of society, the pushing forward to the realization of that dream, that the dynamic of the Kingdom of God provides.

> The future of the Kingdom releases a dynamic in the present that again and again kindles the vision of man and gives meaning to his fervent quest for the political forms of justice and love. The new forms that are achieved will, in contrast with the ultimacy of God's Kingdom, turn out to be provisional and preliminary. They will in turn be called upon to give way to succeeding new forms. Superficial minds might think that the political quest is therefore futile. They fail to recognize that the satisfaction is not in the perfection of that with which we begin but in the glory of that toward which we tend. We possess no perfect program, but are possessed by an inspiration that will not be realized perfectly by us. It is realized provisionally in the ever-renewed emergence of our striving in devotion to history's destiny.[7]

To work for the Kingdom, then, is not to be unrealistic about the flaws in man's nature which always prevent him from realizing his highest ambitions, or to make the fatal mistake of identifying the Kingdom with the essentially provisional and limited character of any political order, ambitions, or party. (Some recent liberation-theologies might be very suspect on this last ground.) Instead, the vision of the Kingdom challenges all our dogmatisms. Through his parables of the Kingdom, Jesus let his hearers feel that such unrestricted discovery and possession and sharing would offend, not only against their anxious, grasping, excluding and hostile instincts, but against the most insistently rationalized and the most solemnly institutionalized prejudices and presuppositions of their culture.[8]

But if our understanding of the Kingdom does not allow it to be subsumed under any particular social programme, it still asks of us a commitment now to 'the provisional', a grubbing about, a 'being earthed' in political realism and local action. To try to bypass such labours because we are committed to the Kingdom is to betray the Kingdom itself. Such a commitment to the provisional does not mean accepting the facile view that betterment of social conditions, and the triumph of one segment of humanity (the blacks, the poor) over another (the whites, the rich) is all that matters. The picture of the Kingdom always reveals more than can be seen at any one glance: there are always deeper needs, more opportunities, wider horizons, greater possibilities to be sought. It is always there to call out more from us – and there will be still more left over. That is the excitement of the Kingdom. It has its own relentless dynamic, and never allows of a shallow optimism, nor of a gloomy pessimism: the coming of the Kingdom does not all depend on us. The farmer in the parable goes out, doing his part of the job, sows the seed, then commits the fields to God and lies down to sleep. That is faith in the Kingdom. Perhaps Mazzini, the saint of the Italian Republic Movement, during the defence of Rome in 1849, unwittingly expressed that faith: 'We must act like men who have the enemy at the gates, and at the same time like men who are working for eternity.' The two attitudes Mazzini describes are not separate, but interrelated. Vision can emerge through struggle, wrestling and involvement. We talk (perhaps inevitably) as if having had the vision in some quiet corner, we go away and do. It is not often like that. The important point is that the struggle should not blur the vision, or the vision lessen the demands of the struggle.

There is, then, a prophetic concern in the pastor's task, a social commitment, but it comes out of and is related to his vision of the Kingdom of God. The pastor will recognize in-

sistent clamorous voices urging him to throw in his lot completely with those political activists who seek to ferment revolution on the grounds that only thus will the welfare of the people
which the pastor has at heart be served. Urban social workers,
angry and frustrated at the injustices of society which seem to
bear so heavily on their clients, are likewise tempted simply to
become militants, spending their time in organizing the tearing
down of the fabric of society rather than doing ambulance-
work, and so perpetuating corruption. But the vision of the
Kingdom is the proper pastoral resource, not because it provides some sort of theological modifying or restraining hand, but
because it provides both realism and hope and does full justice
to the nature of man and his aspirations. In any case, not to
spend time and effort on people now because you are working
for a better future, is to confuse ends and means.

The pastor's political task, then, becomes first the sustaining
of that vision, through his preaching and teaching. At a period
in our national history when there is such a clear political appeal
to self-interest and self-help, the importance of the vision of a
caring society which recognizes that we are our brother's keeper
can hardly be exaggerated. Indeed, the cohesion and perhaps
ultimately the survival of our political system depends upon it.
This is not to imply that the pastor sits above the dust and heat
·of battle, pointing heavenwards. The proper perspective derived
from vision does not lead to inaction, which is simply action of a
particular kind. (The Last Judgment pictures the fate of those
who do nothing.) His role will often be that of animateur: of
bringing together people from different helping professions and
other walks of life to consider and take action over a certain
need, hazard or evil in the community. I do not underestimate
what a difficult and delicate task this is. Professionals quite
rightly view with deep suspicion the worthy attempts of out-
siders to point to a few home truths about their professional
assumptions and aims or to make suggestions as to what they
really ought to be doing. An over-simplistic or ham-fisted approach can retard rather than advance the work of the Kingdom.
Academics feel sceptical when university chaplains start being
'prophetic' about the content of university courses; politicians
are irritated when well-meaning people talk of the simple appli-
cation of 'Christian principles' to policies. To be an 'animateur'

means nothing more perhaps at first than to be a servant, an office-boy. Through his humility and caring approach, he may be able to inspire a group of people who will try to remove the obstacles which frustrate personal fulfilment in the context of community life, and so in this, the pastor will be alongside practitioners in other disciplines. But he will see these goals as preliminaries to the establishment of the Kingdom of God. Again, the pastor has an almost unique opportunity at 'grass-roots level' in the community to observe, for instance, where inflation bites most and where the politicians are missing the real needs of people. Since he will be in touch with local politicians, councillors and his own Member of Parliament, he will be able to make a real contribution both to understanding and to action, which will come out of his day-to-day knowledge of the people amongst whom he moves.

Now if it be objected that such a pastoral approach to political and social action is too 'soft', cutting no ice in the most hopeless of situations, it is worth considering the implications of Carl Rogers' 'person-centred approach' to social problems, and the parallel he found with the revolutionary thinking of Paulo Freire, expressed especially in his *Pedagogy of the Oppressed*. Rogers discovered that the principles of Freire's work with oppressed peasants in Brazil were very similar to those with which he had operated in his counselling and educational work. For instance, the inter-disciplinary team of workers which goes into an area with a high degree of illiteracy and apathy, will aim to be alongside those living there, seeing them from inside, and so building trust and confidence. Just as in India where the low caste and outcaste Christian converts tended to look on the missionaries and the church as patrons, sources of power, money and employment, so the oppressed will always seek a position of dependence on the team (compare the counselling situations: 'tell me what to do'; 'what would you do if you were me?'). All this is resisted in the interests of making the people face their own problems in a way which is appropriate to them. So the issues which the peasants have raised in a tirade of complaints become problems for them to tackle – with dignity. In learning to trust one another, their goals have changed: instead of simply trying to become oppressors in their turn in revenge for their terrible plight, they begin to envisage a more human form of society, and frame action designed to bring what they know in line with it. In his Foreword to *Pedagogy of the Oppressed*, Richard Shaull speaks of the far-reaching implications of Freire's work:

> A distinguished Brazilian student of national development recently affirmed that this type of educational work among the people represents a new factor in social change and development, 'a new instrument of conduct for the Third World, by which it can overcome traditional structures and enter the modern world'.[9]

If that is true of Brazil, it could be even more true of Birmingham. It argues an identification, a sharing with, which has not always been apparent in circles where to be pastoral is to be patronizing. It suggests a most commendable pastoral method in dealing with situations of deprivation. It is to be the silent midwife of a revolution. No wonder that Freire refers to the effect Brazilian peasants have said it has had on them: 'We were blind, now our eyes have been opened.'

There is a lot of loose talk in some theological circles about 'influencing the structures'. It is difficult to resist the feeling sometimes that it is one more insidious step towards the glamorous cult of 'relevance' and 'immediacy'. To take one person's feeling, thought, ambitions and despair seriously and unconditionally is far more demanding than any number of 'social theology' debates and dialogues, yet can never make headlines in the way that some Christian's radical political position may. But, as Freire's work rightly shows, there is no dichotomy between the pastor's stance in counselling individuals and his political and social action. He always stands, in a world where many pressures, not excluding traitors in his own camp, would distract him, for the attempt to vindicate the personal. His attempt will not only be right: however long it takes, it will also in the end, be successful. Under the compulsion of the Kingdom, the pastor will never settle for the impersonal, but always seek the true welfare of the person. There, at least, is pastoral distinctiveness.

8

The Pastor Himself

It is easy to use exalted phrases about the pastor's vocation – and highly dangerous. Some of the worst traits of clerical office, especially condescension, have come from the pedestal on which the pastor has been placed, and the curious aura of fragility and unreality with which he has often been surrounded. To talk, as Gregory the Great does, of the pastor's work being 'the art of arts' is to invite many misconceptions, as does the contrast often drawn in theory but impossible to sustain in practice between magnifying the office but not the man.

Such language inevitably deflects attention away from the pastor himself, and his essential humanity. He needs to recognize his own mixed motivation in becoming a pastor: high-flown language about vocation may blur that recognition which is so essential to the realism with which he faces his work. This is not to deny the *fact* of vocation, that God calls men to particular human responsibilities: it is to ground that vocation in our humanity, the way God has made us. Equally, the pastor will recognize the way in which he is fed sometimes with too rich a diet of flattery, approval, esteem. The parson's social and economic status may have declined almost to vanishing-point in some urban communities, but in the more personal aspects of his ministry, he still needs to keep a sober appreciation of himself in the face of his 'admirers'. He may suffer, too, from the over-confident expectations of some people that he can give all the answers, solve all problems, and that can only lead to an illegitimate sense of pride or intense depression. Further, those qualities of his which are most valuable and most demanding in his work – availability, a willingness to give patiently and freely of time and effort to other people's needs, an intense self-giving – may be just those qualities which will take him away from, and perhaps lead him even to neglect, those nearest to him. That, in turn, may lead him to ignore the most fruitful and painstaking lessons he may have to learn, on his own doorstep. His openness to learning from his relations and closest friends may be a crucial factor if he is to be able as a pastoral artist to articulate what is going on in other people and give it shape. The danger is that those who make themselves available to everyone may find themselves unable to develop closeness to anyone. My own mistake has been to assume that those closest to me will be with me as I make myself available to others, and I have to acknowledge my own blindness to their real needs, which sometimes lie just under my nose.

If he does not experience the adulation of a small coterie, another acute condition from which the pastor may suffer today is isolation and loneliness, burdens still unrecognized in many of the structures of the church, even of those which pride themselves most on their 'episcope'. This condition arises, again, out of the pastor's diminishing impact on society, his marginal position. There is an odd irony about the way in which the pastor's business is with ultimate concerns of life and death, events at the centre of life where the struggle is most intense and poignant, and yet he often finds himself on the touchline in public places. Even in hospitals and prisons, where chaplains have a well-defined pastoral role, pastors sometimes feel like 'optional extras', tolerated (although not always) but in no way significant. There is a loneliness arising from his professional work as pastor, in addition to the inescapable loneliness of the human condition.

Henri J. M. Nouwen in *The Wounded Healer* movingly explores this double pain and loneliness. If, he says, the pastor understands the source of his own pain, he can make the experience of weakness a means of strength, and offer that experience to others who simply face a bleak suffering they cannot understand. This may be harder for him in that he is, in addition, often committed to nourish a community of faith, and hence he will be tempted to deny or neglect his own loneliness. The relationship between his professional and personal life is perhaps more subtle for the pastor than for most of the caring professions. Whilst it may still be possible for a doctor to be good doctor even when his private life is seriously disturbed, the pastor (as we have seen) cannot be of help unless he is acknowledging and using his own inner experiences. It is not that he should parade those experiences either in an orgy of exhibitionism or in the sort of infuriating response to other people's problems which simply says, 'We all suffer from that at some time or another: I know I do!' To use one's wounds as a source of healing is not a matter of 'sharing superficial personal pains' but 'a constant willingness to see one's pain and suffering as rising from the depth of the human condition which all men share'. And this does not 'contradict the concept of self-realization, or self-fulfilment but deepens and broadens it'. [1] Nouwen describes how many words have been used to describe the healing task of the pastor – words like compassion, understanding and forgiveness – but says that the word he prefers is *hospitality*, which has deep roots in the Judaeo-Christian tradition, and provides insight into the way we can respond to human isolation and loneliness. Hospitality

is the virtue which allows us to break through the narrowness of our own fears and to open our houses to the stranger, with the intuition that salvation comes to us in the form of a tired traveller. Hospitality makes anxious disciples into powerful witnesses, makes suspicious owners into generous givers, and makes closed-minded sectarians into interested recipients of new ideas and insights. [2]

Hospitality requires both that the host feel at home in his own house and that he can create a free and open space for the person who 'drops in'. It is by withdrawing into ourselves, not out of self-pity, but out of humility, that we 'can be free to let others enter into the space created for them, and allow them to dance their own dance, sing their own song and speak their own language without fear'. [3] This is healing ministry

because it takes away the false illusion that wholeness can be given by one to another. It is healing because it does not take away the loneliness and the pain of another, but invites him to recognize his loneliness on a level where it can be shared. Many people in this life suffer because they are anxiously searching for the man or woman, the event or encounter, which will take their loneliness away. But when they enter a house with real hospitality they soon see that their own wounds must be understood not as sources of despair and bitterness, but as signs that they have to travel on in obedience to the calling sounds of their own wounds. [4]

So a Christian community becomes a place of healing not because it is the place of those success stories dearly loved of some Christian publicists, where wounds are cured and pains miraculously disappear, but because those wounds and pains become the means of new vision.

The seriousness and delicacy of his work for others, then, his need to articulate what is going on in himself and those around him, and his willingness to make his own wounds sources of healing for others, all point to the same questions: how is the pastor to keep untarnished his own vision, and where is he to find nourishment to sustain him?

At the deepest level, I suspect, this will only happen when he is willing to die a thousand deaths, be the daily victim of a 'minor death'. Here again Iris Murdoch helps us to see that there is a kind of minor death, comparable in biblical terms to wrestling with an angel, or being swallowed by a whale. In her novel *The Unicorn* Effingham Cooper, a successful civil servant, but immature and vain, finds himself caught in a bog, slowly beginning to sink, without any hope of being rescued.

Effingham had never confronted death. The confrontation brought with it a new quietness and a new terror. The dark bog seemed empty now, utterly empty, as if, because of the great mystery which was about to be enacted, the little wicked gods had withdrawn. Even the stars were veiled now and Effingham was at the centre of a black globe. He felt the touch of some degraded gibbering panic. He could still feel himself slowly sinking. He could not envisage what was to come. He did not want to perish whimpering. As if obeying some imperative, a larger imperative than he had ever acknowledged before, he collected himself and concentrated his attention; yet what he was concentrating on was blackness too, a very dark central blackness. He began to feel dazed and light-headed.

Max had always known about death, had always sat there like a judge in his chair facing toward death, like a judge or like a victim. Why had Effingham never realised that this was the only fact that mattered, perhaps the only fact there was? If one had realised this one could have lived all one's life in the light. Yet why in the light, and why did it seem now that the dark ball at which he was staring was full of light? Something had been withdrawn, had slipped away from him in the moment of his attention and that something was simply himself. Perhaps he was dead already, the darkening image of the self forever removed. Yet what was left, for something was surely left, something existed still? It came to him with the simplicity of a simple sum. What was left was everything else, all that was not himself, that object which he had never before seen and upon which he now gazed with the passion of a lover. And indeed he could always have known this for the fact of death stretches the length of life. Since he was mortal he was nothing and since he was nothing all that was not himself was filled to the brim with being and it was from this that the light streamed. This then was love, to look and look until one exists no more, *this* was the love which was the same as death. He looked, and knew with a clarity which was one with the increasing light, that with the death of the self the world becomes quite automatically the object of a perfect love. He clung on to the words 'quite automatically' and murmured them to himself as a charm.

Something gave way under his right leg and it seemed without his will to be straightening out below him. He leaned sideways, thrusting out his hands involuntarily to try to pull himself upward. There was nothing firm, and his hands plunged desperately about in the mud. He became still, lifting his muddied hands to his face. He was now fixed in the bog almost to the waist and sinking faster. The final panic came. He uttered several low cries and then a loud terrified shrieking wail, the voice of total despair at last.[5]

Previously, Effingham Cooper has not been able to perceive other people and things as real and since properly to love is to recognize something besides oneself, he has apparently found it impossible to have a close relationship with anyone. Through his experience of facing the fact of death for the first time he is able to have his eyes opened, and the blindness caused by his self-concern removed. 'Something had been withdrawn, had slipped away from him in the moment of his attention and that something was simply himself.' 'This then was love, to look and look until one exists no more, *this* was the love which was the

same as death.' The key to this 'minor death' is the withdrawal
of any attempt to exercise power or control, the recognition of
the independence of other things. It is a 'letting-go', a willingness to allow other things and other people their full freedom to
be, and so not to have a distorted awareness of them.

Such 'minor deaths', such daily dying to self are, of course,
rooted in the gospel, in Christian tradition and liturgy. This is
no new truth, but one as venerable as the faith itself. But because it is especially applicable to the life of the pastor, perhaps
we need to approach it from a different perspective – if for no
other reason than to keep the old truth fresh enough to bear real
meaning for us. I feel no necessity to apologize for introducing
again the appeal to the literary and aesthetic. A depressing
feature of our education system with its pressure to specialize,
and our career-patterns which force people to conform and
compete, is the way in which we appear to be turning out men
and women who are in some sense 'empty'. (There are many
university students who never read or look at paintings for sheer
pleasure and curiosity.) How can you be whole and empty at
the same time? Peter Shaffer's play, *Equus*, revolving round the
confrontation between a psychiatrist and a boy who has blinded
six horses, is concerned with this emptiness. In spite of his criminal act, it is the boy's *passion* for horses which shows up the
shallowness in the lives both of the psychiatrist and his wife. 'I
settled for being pallid and provincial, out of my own eternal
timidity.'[6] He mocks himself for the way in which he has shrunk
his own life within safe and secure boundaries, giving the impression of a smooth, cultured mature person, but allowing
nothing beyond these boundaries to disturb him or make him
want to stretch the boundaries.

> Such wild returns I make to the womb of civilization. Three
> weeks a year in the Peloponnese, every bed booked in ad-
> vance, every meal paid for by vouchers, cautious jaunts in
> hired Fiats, sponge-bag crammed with Entero-Vioform!
> Such a fantastic surrender to the primitive . . .[7]

His wife is in a worse condition, since she does not even recognize the truth of her condition:

> All my wife has ever taken from the Mediterranean – from
> that whole vast intuitive culture – are four bottles of Chianti

to make into lamps, and two china condiment donkeys labelled Sally and Peppy.[8]

Interestingly, the boy's 'passion' (which the psychiatrist recognizes by another name, 'worship') has not only brought the psychiatrist to a state of self-knowledge. He has also begun to realize the necessity to see in life, depth and the dimension of the 'and more' in a way which although it is framed in a non-Christian context, points again to Ian Ramsey's theological stance. (There is even a reference to 'chip shops'!)

I wish there was one person in my life I could show. One instinctive, absolutely unbrisk person I could take to Greece, and stand in front of certain shrines and sacred streams and say 'Look! Life is only comprehensible through a thousand local Gods. And not just the old dead ones with names like Zeus – no, but living Geniuses of Place and Person! And not just Greece but modern England! Spirits of certain trees, certain curves of brick wall, certain chip shops, if you like, and slate roofs – just, as of certain frowns in people and slouches . . .' I'd say to them – 'Worship as many as you can see – and more will appear!'[9]

There are many poets who point to ordinary things and help us to 'see' them and the world 'charged with the grandeur of God'.[10] A particularly good example is the American poet, the late Theodore Roethke, who saw the world as a place enveloped in glory, worthy of the response of reverence for its mystery, a reverence which transfigures even those sights which are distasteful to us. He condemns that rationalizing spirit which is so concerned to intellectualize that it misses the dimension of holiness, and fails to see the presence of Being itself, even in a garden slug.

Reason? That dreary shed, that hutch for grubby schoolboys! The hedgewren's song says something else.[11]

A mind too active is no mind at all;
The deep eye sees the shimmer on the stone. . . .[12]

He has no wish to moralize on what the deep eye sees: his interest is not in any message that things of creation embody, but just that they *are*. He wants us to see things – and people. He

paints a picture of
    the rock singing, and light making its own silence,
At the edge of a ripening meadow, in early summer,
The moon lolling in the close elm, a shimmer of silver,
Or that lonely time before the breaking of morning
When the slow freight winds along the edge of the ravaged
    hillside,
And the wind tries the shape of a tree,
While the moon lingers,
And a drop of rain water hangs at the tip of a leaf
Shifting in the wakening sunlight
Like the eye of a new-caught fish.[13]

He calls to mind those

    three ancient ladies
Who creaked on the greenhouse ladders,
Reaching up white strings
To wind, to wind
The sweet-pea tendrils, the smilax,
Nasturtiums, the climbing
Roses, to straighten
Carnations, red
Chrysanthemums; the stiff
Stems, jointed like corn,
They tied and tucked, –
These nurses of nobody else.
Quicker than birds, they dipped
Up and sifted the dirt;
They sprinkled and shook;
They stood astride pipes,
Their skirts billowing out wide into tents,
Their hands twinkling with wet;
Like witches they flew along rows
Keeping creation at ease;
With a tendril for needle
They sewed up the air with a stem;
They teased out the seed that the cold kept asleep, –
All the coils, loops, and whorls.
They trellised the sun; they plotted for more than them-
    selves.[14]

Taking care that things are allowed to be what they are intended to be, and in so doing, letting them show forth their *holiness*: this is what Roethke urges. Shortly before he died, in 1963, in an address to a public forum at Northwestern University, Roethke expressed the view that 'everything that lives is holy', and said that the intention of his art was to invoke 'these holy forms of life'. 'One could even put this theologically: St Thomas says, "God is above all things by the excellence of His nature; nevertheless, He is in all things as causing the being of all things." ' So, he concluded, a poetry which comes from seeing and calls upon the 'lovely diminutives' of the world is a poetry which calls upon God. He was no pantheist: he does not see his 'lovely dimunitives' swallowed up in some nebulous unity in which all distinctions are annihilated. They are not important simply because they point to some Ultimate Reality beyond themselves; they *are*, in their own right.

> He managed to win the firmest kind of grip on what is of the very essence of the sacramental principle – namely, that nothing may be a sacrament unless everything is, at bottom, sacramental, and that ours may be considered to be a sacramental universe because, in its every aspect and dimension, it is instinct with that which appears to be *for* man rather than *against* him – which is none other than Being itself.[15]

If 'we are engaged in a new search for the possibility of conceiving the world to be a truly sacramental reality' and that must be true of every pastor, then Roethke is one powerful aid to 'guide the spirit and instruct the imagination of such people as ourselves'.[16]

Roethke is just one example of the sort of creative resource we pastors need. Our contemplative spirit can be fed in a thousand ways: some (but not myself) will find opera, dealing as it does with the archaetypal myths of human experience, especially valuable. Some will be content with silence. What matters is the Spirit which will animate us and keep us aware and properly critical. It is not given to many of us to be contemplatives in the technical sense of the word, but what Nouwen has to say here about the contemplative is equally true of the pastor:

> The contemplative is not needy or greedy for human contacts, but is guided by a vision of what he has seen beyond the

trivial concerns of a possessive world. He does not bounce up
and down with the fashions of the moment, because he is in
contact with what is basic, central and ultimate. He does not
allow anybody to worship idols, and he constantly invites his
fellow man to ask real, often painful and upsetting questions,
to look behind the surface of smooth behavior, and to take
away all the obstacles that prevent him from getting to the
heart of the matter. The contemplative critic takes away the
illusory mask of the manipulative world and has the courage
to show what the true situation is. He knows that he is con-
sidered by many as a fool, a madman, a danger to society and
a threat to mankind. But he is not afraid to die, since his
vision makes him transcend the difference between life and
death and makes him free to do what has to be done here and
now, notwithstanding the risks involved.[17]

It could perhaps be argued that in a makeshift, constantly
changing world, I have set my sights too high, been woefully unrealistic in what I have suggested the pastor should attempt to
be, especially when it is likely also that he will have a church-
structure to 'manage'. We can only measure this by comparing
a parallel profession and situation, and happily for me, a recent
interesting example of this has come to hand. *Fifteen Thousand
Hours: secondary schools and their effects on children*[18] is an investiga-
tion by Professor Michael Rutter and three colleagues into
twelve London comprehensive schools, to discover why some
schools are better than others. They found that whether the
schools are good or bad makes a great difference to the pupils'
lives; it affects their attendance or their truancy, their behaviour
in and out of school, their criminal tendencies and their academic performance. They also discovered a clear answer to the
question as to what it is that makes the school good, and it is
almost embarrassingly old-fashioned. It has to do with none of
those things constantly argued about, and on which so much
energy is spent: where the school is, what its staff/pupil ratio is,
what its buildings are like, or even the intake of academically
bright children. It has to do with what Professor Rutter calls
the ethos of the school, and that in turn depends entirely on the
staff of the school. The teachers should have clear goals, and
faith that their pupils can go some way towards meeting them.

They have high expectations of their pupils and are generous with their praise when they make good progress. Above all, the teachers themselves should set a good example.

But, of course, academic goals are by no means the only ones. Just as important are the goals, and the expectations of successful progress towards them, in the sphere of behaviour. And it is here that the teachers have a vast and perhaps unwelcome responsibilitity. For children *do* learn by example. If teachers are to teach their pupils not only to read and write and calculate and pass their examinations, but also to behave properly, to respect one another and to respect property, to take responsibility and to fulfil obligations, then they must be seen to do all these things themselves. They must be punctual at lessons, conscientious about setting and marking work, everlastingly fair and patient, open to talk to, and actually *like*, their pupils, Nothing less will do. Moreover, in order that a consistent and recognizable ethos should be established in a school, it is essential that teachers should co-operate with one another, and that the senior and experienced teachers should support, and even supervise, the junior and inexperienced.[19]

It is unnecessary to draw out what seems to be a most exact analogy. There is abundant evidence of the importance of vision, of personal goals, the growth that occurs when those goals are not lost sight of, the sharing of pastor and person in similar goals, the cost and great reward of personal involvement and example. Many churches, when looking for a vicar or minister, ask for a 'good pastor'; behind all the superficial misconceptions about the phrase, a person with something of this character and aim is what they seek.

There is a fascinating Hindu idea (at least in Vedanta) that the highest experience in human life is 'realization', and the guru is the man who both displays that realization in himself, and leads others to it. His own realization is the ticket on which others accept his guidance; he has no authority otherwise, no office or function. Again, the parallel seems to be exact. To be nakedly vulnerable with the vulnerability of Christ is our greatest pastoral privilege and asset: this is the simple gift of grace we need. Where are those 'pastores pastorum' who will unlock for us this treasury of the grace of God, and allow those gifts to flow freely?

Notes

Chapter 1

1. V. A. Demant, *The Responsibility and Scope of Pastoral Theology Today*, OUP 1950, p. 5.
2. James Lapsley, *New Shape of Pastoral Theology* ed W. Oglesby, Jnr, Abingdon Press, Nashville 1969, p. 43.
3. C. R. Forder, *Parish Priest at Work*, SPCK 1948.
4. Peter Green, *Town Parson*, Longmans, Green & Co. 1919.
5. George Herbert, *A Priest to the Temple* (1652) ed T. Wood, SPCK 1961, p. 95.
6. Paul Halmos, *The Faith of the Counsellors*, Constable 1965, p. 8.
7. Quoted by David L. Edwards, *Religion and Change*, Hodder & Stoughton 1969, p. 314.
8. David Cecil, *Visionary and Dreamer: Two Poetic Painters*, Constable 1969, p. 45.
9. Simone Weil, *Gravity and Grace*, Routledge & Kegan Paul 1952, p. 106.
10. Iris Murdoch, *The Sovereignty of Good*, Routledge & Kegan Paul 1970, pp. 85–6.
11. Ibid., p. 84.
12. Iris Murdoch, *The Bell*, Chatto & Windus 1958, p. 192.

Chapter 2

1. Kenneth E. Kirk, *The Vision of God*, Longmans, Green & Co. 1931, p. 1; reissued James Clarke 1977.
2. Ibid., p. 96.
3. *Confessions of St Augustine*, Book X, 27; p. 232 in the Penguin 1961 edn.
4. Nicholas of Cusa, *The Vision of God*, Atlantic Paperbacks, New York, p. 24.
5. Simone Weil, *Waiting on God*, Routledge & Kegan Paul 1951, p. 125.

6. A. N. Whitehead, *Science and the Modern World*, CUP 1932, p. 238.
7. John 20.1–9; the discussion of this passage is in Ian T. Ramsey, *Christian Discourse*, CUP 1965, pp. 1–3.
8. Ian T. Ramsey, 'Towards a Theology of Education', in *Launchings* ed John Chapman & Christopher Herbert, Hereford Diocesan Council of Education 1977, p. 24.
9. Ian T. Ramsey, quoted in David L. Edwards, *The British Churches Turn to the Future*, SCM Press 1973, p. 38.
10. *Partners in Education*, National Society/SPCK 1971, p. 79.
11. Ian T. Ramsey in *The Bible Tells Me So*, ed H. Loukes, National Society/SPCK 1967, p. 54.
12. T. G. A. Baker, *Questioning Worship*, SCM Press 1977, p. 8.

Chapter 3

1. Christopher Fry, *A Sleep of Prisoners*, OUP 1951; introductory letter to Robert Gittings.
2. Tom Stoppard, *Jumpers*, Faber & Faber 1972, p. 74.
3. Carl G. Jung, *Integration of the Personality*, Kegan Paul, Trench, Trubner 1940, pp. 290–1.
4. Robert Bolt, *A Man for All Seasons*, Heinemann 1960, pp. xi–xii.
5. H. A. Williams, *The True Wilderness*, Constable 1965, pp. 158–9.
6. Seifert & Clinebell, *Personal Growth and Social Change*, Westminster Press, Philadelphia 1969, p. 68.
7. In *Man's Concern with Holiness* ed Marina Chavchavadze, Hodder & Stoughton 1970, p. 26.
8. Albert Camus, *The Plague*, Hamish Hamilton 1948; Penguin 1960, pp. 208–9.
9. Paul C. Vitz, *Psychology as Religion: the cult of self-worship*, Eerdmans, Grand Rapids 1977, pp. 91, 95.
10. Iris Murdoch, *The Sovereignty of Good*, Routledge & Kegan Paul 1970, p. 101.
11. Ibid., pp. 103–4.
12. John Macquarrie, *Paths in Spirituality*, SCM Press 1972, p. 45.

Chapter 4

1. *Paths in Spirituality*, p. 40.
2. In *Spirituality for Today* ed Eric James, SCM Press 1968, p. 77.
3. P. Teilhard de Chardin, *The Phenomenon of Man*, Collins 1955, p. 31.
4. P. Teilhard de Chardin, *Le Milieu Divin*, Collins 1963, p. 29.
5. John Stewart Collis, *The Worm Forgives the Plough*, Penguin 1975, p. 215.

6. Helmut Thielicke, *How the World Began*, James Clarke 1964, p. 200.
7. *Waiting on God*, p. 5.
8. Albert Camus, *The Outsider*, Hamish Hamilton 1946; Penguin 1961.
9. Albert Camus, *The Fall*, Hamish Hamilton 1957; Penguin 1963.
10. David Anderson, *The Tragic Protest*, SCM Press 1969.
11. Grahame Greene, *The Living Room*, Heinemann 1953, p. 49.
12. Ibid., p. 58.
13. Martin Esslin, *The People's Wound*, Methuen 1970, p. 107.
14. Ibid., p. 235.
15. Carl Rogers, *Encounter Groups*, Penguin 1969, p. 9.
16. Thomas Oden, *Intensive Group Experience*, Westminster Press, Philadelphia 1972.
17. Thomas Merton, *The Wisdom of the Desert*, Hollis & Carter 1960, p. 23.

Chapter 5

1. John A. T. Robinson, *Honest to God*, SCM Press 1963.
2. *The Myth of God Incarnate* ed John Hick, SCM Press 1977.
3. David L. Edwards, *Religion and Change*, Hodder & Stoughton 1969, p. 290.
4. *The Philosophy of Education* ed R. S. Peters, OUP 1973, pp. 112–13.
5. Paul Tillich, *The Shaking of the Foundations*, SCM Press 1949, p. 116.
6. David E. Jenkins, *The Contradiction of Christianity*, SCM Press 1976, p. 85.
7. Ibid., p. 86.
8. In *Aims in Education* ed T. H. B. Hollins, Manchester University Press 1964, pp. 69–70.
9. Harvey Cox, *Seduction of the Spirit*, Wildwood House 1974, p. 323.

Chapter 6

1. Brian Clark, *Whose Life is it Anyway?*, Amber Lane Press 1978, p. 27. Quotations are made by kind permission of the author.
2. Alexander Solzhenitsyn, *Cancer Ward*, Bodley Head 1970, p. 87.
3. Sidney Jourard, *The Transparent Self*, D. Van Nostrand, New York 1971, p. 182.
4. *Whose Life is it Anyway?*, pp. 30–31.
5. Ibid., p. 34.
6. Ibid., p. 54.
7. Monica Furlong, *God's a Good Man and Other Poems*, Mowbrays 1974, p. 62.

8. *Christian Believing*, a Report by the Doctrine Commission of the Chuch of England, SPCK 1976, p. 3.
9. Dietrich Bonhoeffer, *Life Together*, SCM Press 1954; 6th imp 1965, p. 75.
10. Dietrich Bonhoeffer, *Ethics*, SCM Press 1955; rev edn 1971, pp. 103–4.
11. Susan Hill, *In the Springtime of the Year*, Hamish Hamilton 1974.

Chapter 7

1. Letter to an English friend, quoted in Judith M. Brown, *Gandhi and Civil Disobedience*, CUP 1972.
2. C. H. Dodd, *The Parables of the Kingdom*, James Nisbet 1955.
3. Wolfhart Pannenberg, *Theology and the Kingdom of God*, Westminster Press, Philadelphia 1969, p. 54.
4. Ibid., p. 80.
5. Ernest Fischer, *Marx in His Own Words*, Allen Lane 1970, p. 27.
6. Ibid., p. 17.
7. *Theology and the Kingdom of God*, pp. 80–81.
8. James P. Mackey, *Jesus – the Man and the Myth*, SCM Press 1979, p. 141.
9. Paulo Freire, *Pedagogy of the Oppressed*, Penguin 1972, p. 13 (Foreword by Richard Shaull).

Chapter 8

1. Henri J. M. Nouwen, *The Wounded Healer*, Doubleday, New York 1972, p. 90. Copyright © 1972 by Henri J. M. Nouwen.
2. Ibid., p. 91.
3. Ibid., p. 93.
4. Ibid., p. 94.
5. Iris Murdoch, *The Unicorn*, Chatto & Windus 1963, pp. 197–99. Quoted by permission. I am grateful to Professor Diogenes Allen of Princeton University for this illustration.
6. Peter Shaffer, *Equus*, André Deutsch 1973, p. 79.
7. Ibid., p. 79–80.
8. Ibid., p. 60.
9. Ibid., p. 61.
10. See Gerard Manley Hopkins poem, 'God's Grandeur'.
11. Reprinted by permission of the publisher from *The Collected Poems of Theodore Roethke*, Faber & Faber 1968, p. 92.
12. Ibid., p. 244.
13. Ibid., p. 204.
14. Ibid., p. 44.

15. Nathan A. Scott, Jnr, *The Wild Prayer of Longing*, Yale University Press 1971, pp. 117–18. I am grateful to the author for introducing me to this poet.
16. Ibid., p. 118.
17. *The Wounded Healer*, p. 45.
18. Michael Rutter et al, *Fifteen Thousand Hours: secondary schools and their effects on children*, Open Books 1979.
19. Mary Warnock, reviewing *Fifteen Thousand Hours* in *The Listener*, 26 April 1979, p. 587.